D1527447

WORKERS UNDER STRESS

WORKERS
UNDER
STRESS

The Impact of Work Pressure on Group Cohesion

STUART M. KLEIN

UNIVERSITY PRESS OF KENTUCKY
Lexington, 1971

ISBN: 0–8131–1253–2

Library of Congress Catalog Card Number: 75–160046

Copyright © 1971 by The University Press of Kentucky

A statewide cooperative scholarly publishing agency
serving Berea College, Centre College of Kentucky,
Eastern Kentucky University, Kentucky State College,
Morehead State University, Murray State University,
University of Kentucky, University of Louisville,
and Western Kentucky University.

Editorial and Sales Offices: Lexington, Kentucky 40506

Acknowledgments

THE COMPLETION of this study depended upon the insights, encouragement, and effort of a number of people. Special thanks must be extended to those who were particularly helpful from design to interpretation: R. A. Dunnington, Henry Landsberger, Lee Meltzer, Frank Miller, R. Richard Ritti, David Sirota, and William Foote Whyte. In addition, kind thanks are extended to Stanley Seashore, whose classic study on work group cohesion provided the impetus for this study and whose comments on the original draft were exceedingly encouraging.

CONTENTS

Figures

Tables

INTRODUCTION

THE PURPOSE of this study is to examine the impact of industrial work pressures on work group cohesion. Each of these classes of variables must be considered an important aspect of the industrial work scene. Industrial organizations are constantly pushing for increases in performance and reductions in costs. To remain viable in a highly competitive economy they must improve their productive efficiency, and attaining this goal may require the imposition of work pressures on individual workers and work groups. In many studies of group behavior (e.g., Argyris 1964, Klein and Ritti 1970, Likert 1967, and McGregor 1960) work pressure is an important theme. Indeed, observers of industrial organizations must deal with the concept sooner or later, for it is an important aspect of the work-centered environment.

Likewise, studies of work group cohesion have appeared consistently in the literature on organizations. While the early work by industrial psychologists and engineers tended to focus on individual workers, the Hawthorne studies dramatically changed that focus (Roethlisberger and Dickson 1939). These studies underlined the importance of the work group and the social motives pertinent to any social structure by demonstrating that industrial work groups establish informal production norms which are closely followed by the group members. While the Hawthorne studies have come under critical scrutiny recently (Carey 1967), the central criticisms do not question the importance of the group itself but rather a misleading emphasis on leadership and human relations. In fact, the work groups are now recognized as so important that most current textbooks on organizational behavior devote at least a chapter to them. For example, one of the foremost writers in the field devotes six chapters of a recent text to the various dimensions of group dynamics (Whyte 1969).

Participative management and group decision making, an offshoot of the central focus on groups, is still an issue even though the initial studies were conducted in the 1940s. Since then a number of studies focusing specifically on group decision making have appeared; they are best summarized in Likert's two recent books (1961 and 1967) and Vroom's chapter in the *Handbook of Social Psychology* (1969). One theoretical thrust of Likert's current work involves group-oriented management and is based on two decades of group dynamics studies. However, while Likert's 1967 study mentions work pressure and Buck (1963) and Seashore (1954) consider the impact of group cohesion on feelings of work pressure, the reverse causal relationship between the two variables has not been explored. Thus a study of the impact of work pressure on industrial work groups is warranted both because of its significance and because little has been done to relate the two concepts in industrial settings.

A Survey of Group Cohesion Research

During the past three decades a considerable amount of research has been done on both causes and consequences of group cohesion in terms of group members' attitudes and behaviors. For example, Lott and Lott (1965), in a thorough review article, examined only those studies appearing from 1950 through 1962 which focused on the antecedent or consequent relationships of interpersonal attractions; they produced a bibliography of almost 300 published studies. Since 1962 the major programmatic studies have been conducted by the Lotts (Lott, Lott, and Matthews 1969; Lott et al. 1969; Lott and Lott 1966, 1968) and by Byrne and his co-workers (Byrne 1969). Focusing on the antecedents of interpersonal attractions, they use similar reinforcement theory frameworks. A number of doctoral dissertations have also been written on cohesion, although few of them make substantial contributions to the cohesion literature in a systematic way.

Most research on cohesion has been conducted in ad hoc experimental groups or in groups of children; very little has been done with ongoing groups of a relatively permanent nature. A notable exception is the work of Newcomb (1961), who conducted longitudinal studies of college men who were initially strangers and who then were housed together. Looking primarily at the antecedents of interpersonal attractions, Newcomb found that, over time, people with similar attitudes tended to develop closer personal relations, though this function varied according to attitudinal area. This kind of finding has been repeated consistently in the above-mentioned experimental situations as well as in cross-sectional studies using sociometric data as correlates of opinions, attitudes, and values (e.g., Byrne 1969; Lott and Lott 1965).

Industrial work groups, however, have received relatively little systematic attention from those interested in group cohesion. The famous Hawthorne studies underlined the importance of group cohesion and productivity norms. Whyte (1955) and Trist and Bamforth (1951) dealt with this topic as well, though their interpretations were primarily ad hoc and incidental to the main thrust of their studies. But the classic study dealing with antecedents and consequences of group cohesion in the industrial context was conducted by Stanley Seashore in 1954.

The Seashore study was conducted in a company manufacturing heavy machine equipment, and the jobs were largely skilled or semiskilled. Seashore's data were obtained from a questionnaire administered to 5,871 employees who were members of 228 work groups. The measurement of cohesiveness included five items asking the individual employee about others in his work group (Seashore, pp. 36–37). The intercorrelations of these items were at best modest (Seashore, p. 38). The hypotheses that Seashore attempted to test were as follows:

1. Members of highly cohesive groups will exhibit less anxiety than members of low cohesive groups with respect to matters relevant to group activities or group setting. Mostly confirmed.
2. The degree of cohesiveness in a group determines the power of the group to create forces toward uniformity of behavior among its members. Variation in productivity was used as a measurement of effective group standards. Confirmed.
3. In the case of a cohesive group subjected to forces imposed by an external agent and leading to an uncertain or unobtainable goal, the point of equilibrium between forces toward and away from the goal will be a function of the perceived support of the external agent. In other words, whether the productivity standards are high or low for a particular group depends upon whether that group has a favorable or unfavorable opinion of the company. Confirmed.
4. The degree of cohesiveness in a group will be a function of the attractiveness of its members as determined by their prestige. Confirmed.
5. The degree of cohesiveness in a group will be a function of the attractiveness of its members as determined by the degree of similarity among them. Measures of similarity were age and educational level. Not confirmed.
6. The degree of cohesiveness in a group will be a function of opportunities for interaction among its members. Measures of opportunities for interaction were size of group and length of membership. Confirmed.

As one can see, the batting average was high for confirmation of hypotheses. However, the results also show that the degree of unaccounted for variance vastly overwhelms the accounted for variance in most instances. For example, in the first hypothesis the correlation between the degree of anxiety and the degree of group cohesiveness was $-.28$, a figure which is significant at the .001 level of confidence but which nevertheless accounts for less than 9 percent of the total explained variance. Moreover, in Seashore's third hypothesis, while the data consistently support the hypothesis, they are with few exceptions only marginally significant (Seashore, p. 79).

Of the remaining statistical analyses, none shows a correlation that accounts for more than 9 percent of the total variance, even though, considering the great numbers involved, several are statistically significant. This is not to dispute the value of Seashore's work, but it does point up the amount of unaccounted for variance that Seashore, rightly enough, does not discuss since his purpose is to demonstrate cohesiveness as a variable of some unknown power which operates in the industrial work group.

One possible reason that Seashore's results did not show higher correlations is that he failed to define all the important variables affecting group cohesion. In our estimation one such causal variable is threat (in this study, work pressure) from an outside force. Seashore's index of perceived company supportiveness (Seashore, p. 43) includes this variable but does not specify it. Thus there has been a need for research specifying the relationships between threat engendered by work pressure and group cohesion of ongoing industrial work groups. The following study is designed to meet this need.

CHAPTER 1

Work Pressure, Threat, and Group Cohesion: An
Exploration of Relationships among Variables

THE PLAN of this chapter is to develop the major relationship between work pressure and group cohesion. The central thesis is that work pressure constitutes a threat to the members of industrial work groups and therefore will affect the degree of group cohesiveness. The explicit variables are work pressure as an independent variable and group cohesiveness as a dependent variable. However, in order to develop pertinent arguments and deduce hypotheses, we will also use an intervening construct labeled threat; we will be arguing that work pressure constitutes a sufficient threat to affect group cohesion and that without this threat the relationship between the independent and dependent variables would be minimal.

This chapter will be organized in three parts: first, the relationship between work pressure and threat for industrial work groups and their members; second, the relationship between threat and group cohesiveness; and finally, the residual relationship that might exist between work pressure and group cohesiveness without the intervening variable of threat. In developing our thesis, studies that both support and contradict the position that threat has an important effect on group cohesive behavior will be analyzed. As the argument progresses, it will become clear that the variables are interactive and not isolated.

A thorough discussion of both the conceptual and the

operational definitions of our major variables will appear in Chapter 2. Briefly, for the purposes of clarifying the discussion at hand, work pressure will be considered primarily as externally imposed work demands. Threat will be considered a dangerous situation for the members in a group, involving perceptions of potential bodily harm, disruption of friendship patterns, or attacks upon one's ego from a system that has legitimate power both to coerce and to reward. Group cohesiveness will be considered the extent to which psychological forces operate to bind people together in a common purpose. This latter definition ignores much of the complexity of the concept of group cohesiveness, which will be dealt with at length in Chapter 2.

Work Pressure and Threat

When people have been subjected to increased work demands that are hard to meet, they will be threatened in at least two ways that are pertinent to the subject of this study. First, they will be threatened with losing some control over their environment since with the advent of the work pressure, the work pace is defined by agents other than the workers themselves. Most important, by definition those under pressure have to work as fast as they can, which implies that they cannot control their pace. The threat of the loss of environmental control should produce anxiety with regard to control needs. Argyris (1957) documents in some detail findings based on similar reasoning. He discusses how organizational goals served by cost reduction programs conflict with the personal goal of "self-actualization" and therefore are threatening to the workers involved.

The second way in which work pressures are threatening is that employees are faced with the loss of rewards (i.e., salary increases, transfers to better jobs) and are subject to punishments (i.e., threats, chastisements, transfers to lesser jobs, and, in some cases, dismissals) if they cannot meet the new work demands. Thus the employee must protect himself from financial loss, status loss, and admonishment from his supervisor that might result from a productivity level below the accepted standard.

Threat and Group Cohesion

Janis (1958) reports a number of studies conducted during the Second World War showing that in times of stress people seem to band together in more integrated groups than under normal conditions. Brophy (1946), focusing specifically on white seamen's attitudes toward Negro seamen, illustrates roughly the same phenomenon. He found a high correlation between the number of times white seamen shipped with Negro seamen and the degree of favorableness which the white men exhibited toward Negroes. Superficially this was interpreted as a breaking down of previously held attitudes through increasing contacts with the attitude objects. But in further analyzing the results, Brophy found that the degree of change varied from operation to operation within the same ship. For instance, areas relatively isolated from danger produced very little attitudinal change toward Negroes on the part of whites. Most of the changes occurred in operations in which there was a clear danger and survival was partially dependent upon group members cooperating. The social situation in which these men found themselves was a circumscribed one in which new attitudinal norms had to be established in order for them to operate effectively in the face of constant danger. White men who had previously looked upon Negroes unfavorably were forced to depend upon them for survival. This can be interpreted as an increase in group integration, or cohesion, resulting from threat; the change in attitude can be seen as a social by-product.

Further, Grinker and Spiegel (1945) showed the effects on cohesiveness of commonly perceived danger. The members of bomber crews displayed an increasing cohesiveness when they perceived their own safety to depend upon others in the crew. Lanzetta (1955) too showed that there seemed to be an increase in cohesiveness when groups were placed in stressful situations. Leighton (1945), Burnstein and Mc-Rae (1962), and Myers (1962) reported essentially the same findings. Finally, Lott and Lott (1965) reported five additional studies which indicate that commonly perceived threat is directly associated with group cohesion.

There is also some evidence that social needs increase under conditions of stress. In the most definitive statement thus far, Schachter (1959) demonstrates that, very generally, there is an increase in affiliative tendencies under threat and anxiety and moreover that anxiety can be reduced by group activity. He suggests that anxiety produces the need for self-evaluation, comparing oneself to others in a similar anxiety situation. This finding was replicated by Weller (1963). Further, Rabbie (1963) gave frightened subjects information concerning the emotional state of others and found that while they did not want to be in the company of others who were *more* frightened than they, they much preferred the company of others who were just as frightened over those who had little or no fear at all. It appeared that misery liked misery as long as it was not too miserable. Thus there is evidence that work pressure is threatening to employees and serves to evoke certain control, protective, and social needs which may be reduced in the presence of others sharing these needs.

Contradictory Evidence

There is some contradictory evidence, however. For instance, French (1941) created conditions of both threat and frustration in experimentally created groups and ongoing groups. He found that the ongoing groups behaved rather well compared to the newly created groups but that in both cases there was substantial evidence of disintegrative behavior such as bickering, withdrawal, scapegoating, and the like.

Hamblin (1958) investigated the effects of a crisis situation on a group in the absence of a solution to the crisis problem. Twenty-four ad hoc groups experienced the crisis. Four indices of integration—frequency of helping others, self-oriented behavior, frequency of positive and frequency of negative sanctions—showed reliable differences in the behavior of the crisis groups versus that of the control groups. Each of these indices indicated that integration decreased rather than increased as a result of the crisis. People tended to behave in self-oriented ways: they refused to help others and they issued fewer positive and negative sanctions.

Mintz (1951) experimented with a crisis situation that he considered analogous to a theater fire. Subjects were supposed to pull corks from a bottle according to various degrees of rewards and costs and under conditions of individual versus group rewards. His evidence indicates that people react to a crisis situation in a self-protective manner. When they are rewarded for cooperating in terms of both concrete rewards and absence of punishment, they behave in an integrative way. On the other hand, when the possibility of avoiding the threat is coupled with the probability of punishment for those who do not act on the basis of their own self-interests, then there will be group disintegration. In other words, in the face of a threat, if the reward structure is such as to encourage competitive and/or disintegrative behavior, then this is the behavior that will be exhibited.

In Hamblin's experiment, on the other hand, a cooperative solution to the crisis situation could not have been perceived by members of the experimental group. They were unfamiliar with one another and could not predict one another's behavior; moreover, they were faced with stimuli situations that could clearly be met at least partially by self-protective behavior, and the further step of cooperating to meet the threat probably would have required a greater period of time. Thus in the Hamblin study a cooperative solution to the crisis was not available and people in the group acted in a more obvious, self-oriented way.

Pepitone and Kleiner (1957) squarely faced the problem of the effects of stress and frustration on cohesiveness. These investigators defined threat as a probability that the group will sustain a loss in status; given degrees of threat were represented by probability statements of given degrees of loss. Frustration was defined as uncertainty about whether a group could gain a status position; given degrees of frustration were represented by probability statements of given degrees of gaining status. Groups were divided into high and low status teams. Half of the high status teams were threatened by telling them that their chances of losing status were good, and half of the low status teams were frustrated by telling them that their chances of gaining status were poor. Cohesiveness was defined in terms of interpersonal attraction among members of a team. Theoretically, degrees of cohesiveness were stated as some function of the actual or potential need satisfaction obtained by the members of the group as the result of their team experience. It was assumed that given expectations of gain and loss, these degrees were equivalents of potential satisfaction of approach and avoidance needs.

Following this reasoning, Pepitone and Kleiner hypothesized that as threat and frustration are reduced, cohesiveness increases. In other words, of the original high status groups, those with high probability of losing status will show low cohesion, whereas those with low probability of losing status will show higher cohesion. Likewise, of the original low status groups, those with high probability of gaining status will show high cohesion, whereas those with low probability of gaining status will show low cohesion.

The results show that low probability of status loss leads to higher cohesion than does high probability of status loss. This finding is consistent with the hypothesizing. However, the groups which were given the threat condition were originally high performing groups, which is implied by the definition of status in this experiment. They were told by the experimenters that they were going to lose their performing powers and thereby lose status. Their ability to do anything about these losses was quite beyond the limitation imposed by the experimental design, much as in Hamblin's experiment. It was a situation in which any kind of response, group or individual, was useless—a situation not conducive to cohesive behavior. On the other hand, in the high status groups that were to continue in high status, the situation was a completely pleasant one. As a consequence everything associated with the situation (e.g., other group members), with the task itself, with the experimenters, and so on could be expected to acquire secondary reinforcing characteristics. Because of the way this experiment was structured it is not surprising that the results were consistent with the experimenters' hypothesizing.

Thus the studies that at first glance seem to contradict the empirical investigations reported earlier really do not. In each of the three last-mentioned experiments the experimenters precluded the possibility of successful joint behavior to maintain or to achieve group goals. Presumably a group which discovers that cooperative behavior cannot avert threat or achieve important goals will behave in much the same way as these experimental groups did—namely, show a decrease in cohesiveness. When members of the group cannot see group action, or cohesive behavior, as an effective way of satisfying their needs, or if they perceive that they can better satisfy their needs by individual action, then the degree of cohesion will decrease since cohesive behavior is only one class of behaviors available to them. It is only when the cohesive behaviors are perceived as effective in reducing threat that they will be invoked. Cohesive behavior can be predicted on the basis of its instrumentality in satisfying collective needs.

Work Pressure and Group Cohesion

There is some evidence to suggest that members of cohesive groups can withstand stressful conditions better than members of loosely structured groups (Stouffer et al. 1949; Schein 1956). Seashore (1954) found that cohesive groups felt less work pressure than did noncohesive groups when objective pressure was equal. Buck (1963) found a negative relationship between cohesiveness among first-level supervisors and the amount of pressure that they felt.

Each of these studies used cohesiveness as an independent

variable to predict feelings of pressure. None considered the effects of varying amounts of objective pressure on group cohesiveness, but in the light of the evidence that feelings of pressure are in fact affected by cohesiveness, one would suspect that cohesiveness is an adaptive response that tends to reduce feelings of pressure.

Summary

Most of the evidence indicates that a shared threat to members in a group leads to greater cohesiveness. Specifically, if threat-reducing responses are collectively available to group members, work pressure may constitute a threat to the satisfaction of certain needs, and while feelings of work pressure may be negatively associated with the degree of cohesiveness, there is ample evidence that increasing cohesiveness may be an adaptive response to work pressures that reduces feelings of pressure and satisfies certain needs. Since this is a reinforcing condition one would expect the group under pressure to become increasingly cohesive. Thus we find that a two-step process may occur when work pressure is applied in the industrial context. First, anxiety may be aroused with regard to the satisfaction of certain classes of needs; this is considered threatening to the individual. Second, group cohesiveness may be perceived as an instrumental condition which will satisfy these needs and therefore reduce the imposed threat. We will proceed from these assumptions.

CHAPTER 2

Theory and Hypotheses: An Instrumental Position

SEVERAL AUTHORS consider group behavior as instrumental in achieving individual goals or need satisfaction. For instance, Cartwright and Zander (1968), are instrumentalists who believe that groups can satisfy two classes of needs: when the group itself is the object of the need and when the group is a means of satisfying outside needs.

Bass (1960) considers groups as rewarding collections of people. Two of his major variables are effectiveness (i.e., how rewarding group membership is to individual members of the group) and attraction (i.e., the extent to which the reward for membership is anticipated by individual members). Cohesiveness is a consequent variable that results from the extent to which the member perceives rewards as coming from the group. This is a neat way of stating what the Lotts (1960, 1961, 1965, 1969) call the expectation response: through past rewarding experience in the group a person anticipates satisfaction or dissatisfaction, and this determines the extent to which he is attracted to the group. This position is somewhat different from the instrumental one. Attraction to the group depends upon the amount of reward already achieved in the group (or groups in general) but does not necessarily involve the perception of the group as instrumental in achieving individual goals. However, Bass as well as Cartwright and Zander considers the source of attraction itself to be a rewarding condition of the group.

Homans (1961) thinks of group behavior as a class of variables which is a function of a stimulus-response-reward sequence—basically an instrumental position. The framework is a social situation in which interaction is thought of as individual X's activity stimulating individual Y's activity. If individual Y's activity is rewarded, there will be a greater probability for its occurring again in the presence of similar stimuli; if the activity is negatively reinforced, the probability of its recurring is less. Finally, in keeping with the instrumentalist tradition, there is a point of cessation at which the rewards are no longer worth the cost of performing the activity. At this point Homans invokes the language of economics and talks about profits, or net rewards. Behavior will depend on one's expectation of total net profit or, in Homans's terminology, the extent to which rewards and costs are perceived as being distributed judiciously. Thus if individual X and individual Y perceive mutual benefits as the net result of a particular type of interaction, they will behave accordingly. Thibaut and Kelley (1959) use a similar theoretical structure in which interpersonal attraction is a function of rewards received and costs incurred vis-à-vis others.

Thus we have four similar positions, each describing a social behavior in terms of rewards and costs with expectations about outcomes as a central variable. Our conception of the conditions of group cohesiveness will also be based on the expectation of rewards. It should be noted that from a general theoretical point of view, the theory advanced here is quite similar to the expectancy theory advanced by Vroom (1964) and applied specifically to motivation of organizational managers by Porter and Lawler (1968). Basic to this position is that individuals will act according to their perceptions of the consequences of their acts which in the main will be self-serving.

Since we are dealing with reported group-oriented behaviors, these behaviors themselves will constitute the rewarding condition from which the hypothetical construct, group cohesion, will be deduced. They will be considered instrumental acts in reaching goals that could not be reached as well or at all by individually oriented behavior. The goals will be need satisfaction and the alleviation of threats created by work pressures. This concept is illustrated schematically in Figure 1.

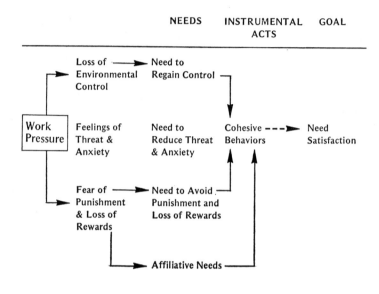

Figure 1
Theoretical Scheme Relating Independent, Contingency,
and Dependent Variables

Conceptual Definition of the Variables
Work Pressure and Group Cohesion

Work Pressure

The work pressures that we deal with here are externally caused and emanate from environmental cues, such as behavior of superiors or company directives. Specifically, the degree of work pressure will be the degree to which the members of the group find it difficult to meet newly introduced workload increases. The new work expectations, if easily met, should provide little in the way of work pressure, but those which are difficult or impossible to meet should provide a great deal of work pressure.

Buck (1963) defines pressure as "a psychological state that exists when the individual perceives (1) conflicting forces and incompatible demands being made on him, (2) at least one of these forces as being 'induced,' (3) the forces as being recurrent or stable over time. Job pressure is that pressure which results from induced forces having their origin in concern about the individual's relationship to his job." We are not concerned with the individual worker's "psychological state" as such, even though this is important. Rather, we are concerned with the objective "induced forces" of productivity demands that are defined by management. Basically we will consider pressure to be identical with the exigent productivity demands in a work group. The exigency of the demands will be considered to vary positively with the percentage of people in the group who cannot meet the demands. A precise operational definition of work pressure will be offered later.

Group Cohesion

Two major conceptual definitions of group cohesion are found in the literature. First, Festinger et al. (1950) state that cohesiveness is the "resultant of all forces acting on each of the members to remain in the group." Cartwright and Zander (1960) elaborate on this definition, stating that the "forces" are consequence of the interaction of the group members' need states and the extent to which the members perceive the group as a source of pertinent need satisfaction. This argument implies that the strength of the "forces" varies with the strength of the interactive effect produced by the need state of the group membership and the characteristics of the group itself which are pertinent to that need state.

Second, Bernice and Albert Lott (1961, 1965), working from a behavioral viewpoint, define cohesiveness as "that group property which is inferred from the number and strength of mutual positive attitudes among the members of a group." (See Byrne 1969 for a similar theoretical statement.) The Lotts go on to state that these attitudes have a drive component.[1] Since they are formed because of a reinforcement of some sort for each member of the group in the presence of all other members, each member will in turn be driven to maintain the acquired secondary reinforcing qualities of every other member.

These two conceptualizations are more similar than dissimilar. Both depend upon the rewarding characteristics of the group itself for its members. If people are rewarded in a group context, then presumably they will have a positive "valence" for that group. At the same time each member of the group should acquire secondary reinforcing characteristics for every other member. Both of these will make the group, or a generalized counterpart, more attractive and productive of forces keeping people in the group. Moreover, the magnitude of the reward should depend upon the need state of the members and the degree to which the group reduces or gratifies these needs or promises gratification.

In this study cohesiveness will be considered as a hypothetical construct which can be inferred from very specific individual behaviors occurring in the group context. We will deal primarily with these behaviors, which result from common needs created by an environmental condition and which constitute the kinds and degree of rewards or need gratification that lead to the construct group cohesion. The major environmental condition is work pressure; the needs are protection against and accommodation to the threat imposed by work pressure; and the behaviors are cooperation, mutual supportiveness, and friendliness, all conducive to the creation of "forces," or "mutual positive attitudes," which are, or lead to, group cohesion.[2]

---

[1] This follows Doob's definition and theoretical statement of attitudes (1947). Doob states that attitudes are implicit responses that have both cue and drive properties. Lott and Lott (1960) substantiated this statement in an experiment. They found that people were rewarded in the presence of others; these others acquired secondary reinforcing characteristics in that they acted as stimuli which evoked an "expectative" goal response. This response is equivalent to the drive properties postulated by Doob.

Hypotheses

We have suggested that work pressure leads to loss of environmental control. This happens because those subjected to work pressure can no longer set their own pace or participate in determining the optimum level of productivity. Moreover, because of the nature of the pressure program in our study, productivity standards were based on predetermined work methods over which the worker had little say. Most important, perhaps, he may have lost the ability to influence his manager with regard to his work. Whatever he does or says makes little difference because the goals are predetermined and inflexible. In addition we suggested that work pressure produces anxiety (fear) with regard to actual level of productivity.

These two assumptions will be tested before we proceed in testing hypotheses since in a sense they can be considered analogous to tests for the effects of "experimental manipulation." Each will be considered contributory to the overall arousal of the needs that can be satisfied through group cohesive behavior.

Assuming that work pressure creates needs and that cohesive behavior can serve to reduce these needs, we make Hypothesis 1: The more the work pressure, the more the cohesive behavior.

The length of time under pressure should be an important variable conditioning the relationship between work pressure and cohesive behavior. If the pressures are newly introduced, they may be perceived as a passing phenomenon

---

[2] Festinger et al. (1950) state that people want to belong to a group because cooperative action can get results that individual action cannot get or because the social interactions are rewarding for their own sake. Fouriezos, Hutt, and Guetzkow (1950) and Deutsch (1953) report higher cohesiveness as measured by feelings of friendliness and satisfaction with the group when members cooperated on group tasks than in those groups in which members primarily exhibited individually oriented behavior. These reports suggest another way of looking at cohesiveness that Lanzetta (1955) calls group integration, or the tendency to build harmony and reduce conflict among group members. In this sense group integration and group cohesiveness are similarly the consequences of group members' behaviors.

requiring no remedial action. If, however, they are in effect a long time, they may be seen as a more immutable and hence threatening factor. In addition time provides the opportunity to experience the rewards of collective action. These assumptions are the basis for Hypothesis 2: The longer under work pressure, the more the cohesive behavior.

Another situation which increases the need for collective action occurs when individual action is felt to be relatively futile in the face of work pressure. If the worker can effectively influence his productivity requirements through personal control over output—getting the requirements changed by appealing to management or causing cessation of the work pressure by making the appropriate goal response—the needs created by the work pressure should be less intense and consequently less productive of cohesive behavior. Thus when work pressure is accompanied by high amounts of "say" over speed and methods (hereafter referred to as "job control"), by responsive management in regard to complaints about "too much work" (hereafter referred to as "effective grievance channels"), or by stable goals that when reached will not further increase (hereafter referred to as "stable standards"), there should be less cohesive behavior. Each of these variables will be considered as a conditioner of the relationship between work pressure and cohesive behavior. (They may have independent effects as well, which we will also consider.) These variables are the basis for Hypothesis 3: the less job control people have, the more the cohesive behavior; Hypothesis 4: the less effective the grievance channels, the more the cohesive behavior; and Hypothesis 5: the less stable the standards, the more the cohesive behavior.

CHAPTER 3

Population Studied and Method Used

THE INDUSTRIAL SETTING for this study offered a unique opportunity to examine the effects of work pressures in industrial work groups. There are two reasons for this. First, the work pressures were newly introduced. The history of employee relations in the company under study was characterized by the slogan, "A fair day's work for a fair day's pay." However, management concluded that in fact the company was not getting a fair day's work from its employees when they compared the production pace to that of other organizations doing similar kinds of work. Up to that point employee performance had been measured against estimates called "past actuals," or the average historical output for each kind of job. When new jobs were introduced, the industrial engineers would study them not with a stopwatch but rather in terms of their similarity to past jobs and would reach an estimate that was to a large extent based upon average past output for similar types of operations. Then things changed.

A consulting firm of industrial engineers estimated that if the company's plants were measured against standard data based on time and motion studies, these plants would be shown to be producing at approximately 60 percent of the average rate. The company adopted the use of these standard data and set to work vigorously to apply them to the individual operators.

A number of people were not yet on the new standard at the time of this study. Moreover, those on the new standard had been on it for varying lengths of time, and the severity of the change also varied. Thus the population under examination could be broken into groups representing various lengths of time under pressure and various degrees of pressure.

The second reason that this industrial population offered a unique opportunity to investigate the effects of pressures on group cohesion is that historically the average employee has maintained a pronounced allegiance to the company. It has in fact been a strong reference group for most of its employees, judging from a comparison between the results of attitude surveys conducted there and in other organizations.[1] Thus a natural conflict of reference groups is a possible consequence of the changed relationship between employer and employee.

The parent corporation has been a historic leader in employee relations. Management has prided itself on establishing pioneer benefits and maintaining high wages. Foremen are warned to respect the sanctity and uniqueness of the individual, and wages are above the industrial norm. The company is not unionized.

The Research Population

The research was carried on in six plant locations across the nation. Three of the plants were located in the Northeast. One was in a border state, one was in a midwestern

---

[1] Until the standards, or work measurement, program was installed, nearly 65 percent of the respondees to the question "How would you rate this company as a place to work compared to other companies you know about?" said "One of the best." Less than 1 percent thought it was below average and about 10 percent indicated a neutral feeling. Herzberg et al. (1957) reported that an absolute minimum of 13 percent of the workers in fifty studies reported in the satisfaction literature indicate dissatisfaction with the companies and that about one-third indicate a neutral feeling. Thus in other companies almost half of the employees responded in a negative or neutral way, whereas in the corporation under study only 11 percent of the response was negative or neutral.

state, and one was in a far western state. The total population comprised more than 17,000 employees, and the size of the plants varied from about 400 to 7,000 employees. They were for the most part blue collar people with skills ranging from semiskilled to very highly skilled. Only the blue collar people were included in this study. All the blue collar people in the smaller plants were used, while in the two largest plants one-third of the blue collar populations were selected by a stratified random sample. Altogether, 3,604 employees were included in the research population.

Data Collection and Analysis

The data were collected over a two-year period. In 1961 a survey was conducted in five locations. The instrument of measurement was the same in all plants that took this survey, which was designed partly by the author of this study and partly by another member of the research staff. A 1962 survey, conducted in a new location and designed solely by the author of this study, duplicated about 50 percent of the items in the 1961 survey; it constitutes a replication and extension of the earlier study. The population of the replication survey was roughly comparable to the first population but different in the kinds of work pressures to which it was subjected.

In each case, a paper-and-pencil, fixed-alternative ques-tionnaire based on forty-eight tape-recorded interviews and three pre-test questionnaires was used.[2] The questionnaires were filled out on company time in large rooms in groups of from 45 to 350 at a time in the presence of members of the research staff. The respondees were completely anonymous: no census data were gathered and identification was by de-partment only. It was impossible to identify an individual respondee.

[2] The interviews and the three pre-tests were administered to randomly selected subjects and were conducted by members of the research staff. The interviews were exploratory and varied from one to three hours depending on the loquaciousness of the subject being interviewed. The pre-tests were administered in surroundings similar to those of the final administration of the questionnaire.

Measurement of Variables

Group Cohesiveness

This variable was measured by the following item:

How many of the people in your department do you think do the following things? CHECK ONE IN EACH LINE ACROSS:

	ALL of them do this (1)	MOST of them do this (2)	SOME of them do this (3)	A FEW of them do this (4)	NONE of them do this (5)
A. Stick up for each other					
B. Are friendly toward each other					
C. Try to work faster than each other					
D. Help each other out on the job					

Work Pressure

This variable was defined by operators' responses to the question whether they had been asked to increase the amount of work they did during a fixed period of time. They also were asked whether or not they felt that they had been able to meet these new expectations. The items were as follows:

Within the last two years, have *you* been required or asked to increase the amount of work you do? (Do *not* count temporary increases due to special jobs.)
CHECK ONE:
1. Yes, I have been required or asked to do more work
2. No, I have not been required or asked to do more work

When first expected to increase the amount you do, were you able to increase it to what you thought was expected of you?

CHECK ONE:
1. Yes, I was able to do this
2. No, I was not able to do this

The degree of work pressure was ascertained by multiplying the percentage of people who had been asked to increase their production by the percentage of people who could not meet the new work expectations.

Job Control

This variable was measured by the two items which follow:

How much "say" do you think you yourself usually have in deciding the *amount* of work you should do on your job? (We know that you cannot be certain about this, but we would like your best guess.)

CHECK ONE:
1. Usually have a great deal of say
2. Quite a bit of say
3. Some say
4. Just a little say
5. Usually have no say at all

How much "say" do you think you yourself usually have in deciding what *methods* you use on your job? (We know that you cannot be certain about this, but we would like your best guess.)

CHECK ONE:
1. Usually have a great deal of say
2. Quite a bit of say
3. Some say
4. Just a little say
5. Usually have no say at all

Degree of Fear

This variable was measured by the following item:

People have different reasons for doing well in their work. How important is each of the following reasons for you? CHECK ONE IN EACH LINE ACROSS:

	VERY IMPOR- TANT (1)	QUITE IMPOR- TANT (2)	FAIRLY IMPOR- TANT (3)	OF LITTLE IMPOR- TANCE (4)	OF NO IMPOR- TANCE (5)
A. I am afraid of being dismissed					
B. I am afraid of being criticized by my manager					
C. I am afraid of being demoted to a lower skilled job					

Grievance Channels

This variable was measured by the following two items:

Suppose your manager required a number of employees in your department to do *more work than was fair.* Listed below are several things an employee in this group might do. For *each* of these, indicate if you think doing this would help. CHECK ONE IN EACH LINE ACROSS:

	Yes, this *definitely* would help (1)	*Yes,* this *probably* would help (2)	*No,* this *probably* would *not* help (3)	*No,* this *definitely* would *not* help (4)
A. Take it up with his manager again				
B. If necessary, take it up with higher management in the plant				

Suppose your manager required a number of employees in your department to do *more work than was fair.* And suppose one of these employees, after complaining to your manager, took his complaint to higher management. Do you think this employee

would be hurt later on for doing this (such as getting the less desirable jobs in the department or being held back on salary increases, or being "picked on," etc.)? CHECK ONE:
1. Yes, he definitely would be hurt for doing this
2. Yes, probably
3. No, probably not
4. No, he definitely would not be hurt for doing this

Stable Standards

This variable was measured by the following two items:

Suppose that during the next month or two you did *more* work than your manager asked you to do. Answer *each* of the following two questions regarding what you think your manager would then do.

Would your manager ask you to do *still more?* CHECK ONE:
1. Yes, he definitely would ask me to do still more
2. Yes, probably
3. No, probably not
4. No, he definitely would not ask me to do still more

Would your manager begin to expect more work from other employees in the department? CHECK ONE:
1. Yes, he definitely would begin to expect more work from others
2. Yes, probably
3. No, probably not
4. No, he definitely would not begin to expect more work from others

The items measuring each variable were combined in indices in order to overcome somewhat the unreliability of single items. All other variables introduced into the analysis will be described in full as we deal with them.

CHAPTER 4

Analysis of Data and
Tests of Hypotheses

THIS CHAPTER will analyze the data obtained from the 1961 study. The 1962 study will be treated in a separate section. We will test each hypothesis and discuss the results in turn.

Before we test the hypotheses, we will attempt to dimensionalize our concept of cohesive behavior. If the cohesive behaviors fall into two or more classes, we will better understand the relationships between work pressure and these behaviors by looking at each relationship separately. In order to do this, three separate analyses were performed: a correlational analysis of individual raw scores, a correlational analysis of the mean scores of the work groups, and a factor analysis of the mean scores of the groups.

The data obtained are part of the larger correlational and factor analyses which included a substantial number of items from the study. Only the results of the four cohesive behavior items are presented below. The Pearson product moment correlation was used.[1]

The matrix indicates moderate correlations among three of the four items used to measure cohesive behavior. People who say that other members in the group tend to "stick up for each other" are also likely to say that others in the group will be friendly and help one another on the job. The item which does not seem to relate to the others is the one asking how many people "try to work faster than each other."

TABLE 1

CORRELATIONAL ANALYSIS USING

INDIVIDUALS AS THE UNIT OF ANALYSIS

How many people in your department do you think do the following things?	A	B	C	D
A. Stick up for each other		.36	−.07	.41
B. Are friendly to each other			−.06	.44
C. Try to work faster than each other				−.12
D. Help each other out on the job				

N = 3,604 production workers

The results by group are almost identical to the results by individual, except that the correlations increase:

TABLE 2

CORRELATIONAL ANALYSIS USING THE WORK

GROUP AS THE UNIT OF ANALYSIS

How many people in your department do you think do the following things?	A	B	C	D
A. Stick up for each other		45	−.10	52
B. Are friendly to each other			−.01	61
C. Try to work faster than each other				−15
D. Help each other out on the job				

N = 172 production departments

Factor analysis results resemble the correlational analysis. Three of the four items are in fairly strong contingency with one another on a factor which can best be labeled "cohesiveness factor," while Item C has a −.08 loading on this factor and therefore is not in strong contingency with the others.

---

[1] The Pearson product moment correlation (r) is used henceforth whenever correlations are presented, with one specified exception.

TABLE 3

FACTOR ANALYSIS USING THE WORK GROUP
AS THE UNIT OF ANALYSIS*

How many people in your department do you think do the following things?	Cohesive Factor	
A. Stick up for each other	.53	.06
B. Are friendly to each other	.64	.04
C. Try to work faster than each other	−.08	.55
D. Help each other out on the job	.64	−.16

N = 172 production departments
* Ten rotations; only first loadings reported. See Appendix A for a detailed description of how this analysis was performed.

The evidence suggests that three of the behaviors lie in contingency with one another but that competitive behavior has little or no linear relationship with the other three. Assuming that these behaviors contribute to an overall effect called group cohesion, it is reasonable to state that group cohesion does consist of different behaviors which may have different consequences. Since competitive behavior seems to be associated with a different class of behaviors, having little or no relationship with the social-supportive or cooperative behaviors, we can assume that people can compete against others in a group without affecting behaviors such as "friendliness" or "cooperativeness." How competitive behavior affects the total "forces" making people want to remain in a group or their "mutual attitudes" toward each other is open to question. It is probable that such effects depend largely on other circumstances. We will deal with some of the possible circumstances later.

With these results in mind the majority of the analyses will be used to test our hypotheses, using a cohesive behavior index which comprises the three related behaviors. In addition we will test the effects of these variables on "competitive" behavior.

Relationships between Work Pressure and Threat

Before testing our hypotheses we will see if work pressure has the expected effects of reducing environmental control and creating anxiety or threat with regard to productivity. In order to test the first effect we correlated our work pressure index against three variables which can be considered to contain elements of environmental control since they involve the employee's ability to influence his environment. They are job control, grievance channels, and stable standards. The product moment correlation coefficients were respectively −.51, −.43, and −.61. Thus work pressure is negatively associated with our measures of environmental control.

To test the second effect we constructed an index comprising the three "fear" items and correlated this index with the pressure index. The coefficient of .59 supports the assumption that work pressure is associated with threat.

Testing the Hypotheses

Procedure

A pool of 172 departments met the criterion of doing production labor. Of these 172 departments, only 150 were selected for this analysis because clear demarcations between pressure groups were desired. Often in surveys, groups are arbitrarily divided at the mean scores to create high and low breaks, and the groups that fall around the mean are not clearly differentiated from each other. Therefore we decided to use a buffer zone between the pressure groups to make the demarcation clearer. This is an arbitrary action, and it leads to certain difficulties.

For one thing, the essentially continuous nature of the variable is lost. Thus a direct correlational analysis between the two variables, work pressure and cohesion, becomes a questionable technique, and other statistical analyses should be performed. In addition we have no idea of how the twenty-two eliminated departments behave in regard to work pressure and cohesive behavior. However, we believe that the advantages of getting clearer distinctions on the independent variable outweigh the drawbacks of these somewhat arbitrary manipulations.

The 150 departments were broken into three pressure groups labeled high, medium, and low pressure. Recall that the pressure index is obtained by multiplying the percentage of people who were asked to increase their productivity by the percentage of people who were not able to do so. The range of percentages was from 70 percent to zero. The high pressure group comprised the 50 departments with the highest percentage of people who could not meet the new work expectations. The low pressure group comprised the 50 lowest departments on this index. The middle pressure group was selected by first computing the mean percentage on the index of the remaining departments and alternately choosing the departments first immediately above and then immediately below this mean, moving away from the mean, until 50 departments were selected.

The range of the percentage of people in the high pressure group who could not meet the work expectations was between 23 percent and 70 percent, with a mean of 34 percent; the range of the middle pressure group was between 10 percent and 19 percent, with a mean of 16 percent; and the range of the low pressure group was between 0 percent and 6 percent, with a mean of 2 percent. Thus a buffer zone was established between each of these groups, though the differences between the high and the low in each group is perhaps not as great as we would have desired.[2]

As mentioned, the index of cohesive behavior comprised

[2] This "objective" measure of work pressure was checked against an item in the questionnaire which read: "How do you feel about the amount of work you are expected to do?" Thirty-six percent of the group defined as "high pressure" according to our index responded "too much." In the middle pressure group 21 percent responded "too much," and in the low pressure group 12 percent responded "too much." This is a clear and high association between our index and "feelings of pressure." In addition we checked our measure against an independent assessment of which departments were subjected to the work measurement program and found that 94 percent of our high pressure groups were under the program, whereas 64 percent of our medium pressure groups and 44 percent of our low pressure groups were under the program. Thus we believe that our measure of pressure is valid.

the three related items while competitive behavior was analyzed separately. The correlation between competitive behavior and the cohesive behavior index was −.14. Mean scores of the cohesive behavior index were computed for each of the pressure groups, as were the scores on the competitive item.

Hypothesis 1: The More the Work Pressure, the More the Cohesive Behavior

To test Hypothesis 1, an analysis of variance was performed to find the degree of association between work pressure and cohesive behavior and that between pressure and competitive behavior. (Details of all statistical analyses are in Appendix B.) The findings are shown in Figures 2 and 3.

It is clear that the hypothesis is not confirmed. If anything, there is a slight negative correlation between work

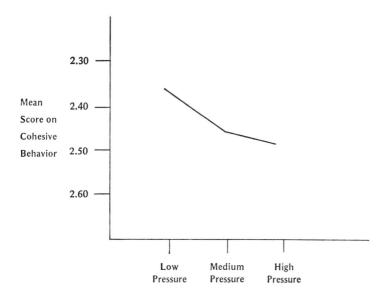

Figure 2
Relationship between Work Pressure
and Cohesive Behavior (F=3.30, P<.05)

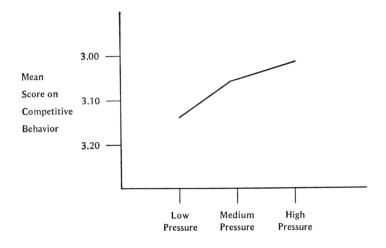

Figure 3
Relationship between Work Pressure
and Competitive Behavior (F=2.51, P<.10)

pressure and group cohesive behavior. The fact that the relationship is significant (P < .05) is due mostly to the high
cohesive behavior of those groups which are under little or
no pressure. There is no difference between the high and
the medium pressure groups in this index.

Competitive behavior is positively related to work pressures, though not significantly (P < .10). Thus both cohesive and competitive behavior operate in an opposite
manner from the one predicted. The more the work pressure, the less the cohesive behavior.[3]

*Hypothesis 2: The Longer under Work Pressure, the More
the Cohesive Behavior*

Only the high and middle pressure groups were used to
test this hypothesis because the low pressure group, with an

[3] See Appendix C for the graphs illustrating the relationship between work
pressure and each of the cohesive behaviors separately. All the relationships
are significant at beyond the .05 level, with the high cohesive behavior of the
low pressure groups producing the main effect.

average of only 2 percent responding that they were asked to increase their work, was inappropriate.

The groups were divided into long and short periods under pressure according to their mean scores on the following item:

About when were you *first* required or asked to increase the amount of work you do?
CHECK ONE:
1. Between one and two years ago
2. Between six months and one year ago
3. Between one month and six months ago
4. Less than one month ago

The responses were checked against objective data compiled by industrial engineers which designated the date that these departments went onto the new standard. Since the correlation coefficient between the questionnaire item and the objective data was .79, we believe that the item is a valid measurement of the length of time under work pressure. The objective data themselves were not used because they applied only to departments on the new standard, which constituted only two-thirds of the total population and consequently would have cut down our pool of departments substantially.

Two computations were performed to test Hypothesis 2. First the mean scores of the two time groups were computed and compared. Next the pressure groups were broken into long and short times under pressure, and two comparisons were made: the first between the high and the medium pressure groups under conditions of long and short times under pressure; the second with each of the two groups, between those who had been under pressure a long time and those who had been under it a short time. The results are shown in Figures 4 and 5.

There is little difference between those under pressure a long time and those under pressure a short time in terms of their cohesive behavior. If anything, there is a slight tendency for those under pressure a long time to behave less cohesively than those under pressure a short time, though this difference

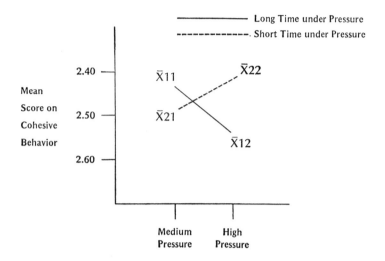

Figure 4
Relationship between Work Pressure and
Cohesive Behavior Controlling for Length of Time
under Pressure (t12,22=1.73, P<.10; all other
differences are not significant*)

*The convention from now on will be to report
only significant relationships.

is not significant. Moreover, the differences between the high and medium pressure groups with both long and short times under pressure are not significant.

However, the relationships between degrees of pressure are different under each of the time conditions. When people have been under pressure a long time, there is a negative relationship between pressure and cohesion. When they are under pressure a short time, there is a positive relationship between pressure and cohesion which is consistent with the kind of relationship hypothesized. Under high pressure the difference between the groups under pressure a long time and those under pressure a short time approaches significance. That is, the longer under pressure when pressure is high, the less the cohesive behavior.

Time seems to make little difference insofar as competi-

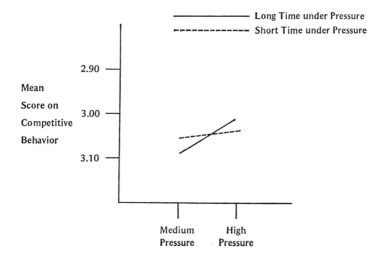

Figure 5
Relationship between Work Pressure and
Competitive Behavior Controlling for
Length of Time under Pressure

tive behavior is concerned. When pressure has been present a long time, there is a stronger positive relationship between competitive behavior and pressure, but the difference in mean scores is not significant.

Thus far the results are mostly contrary to our original predictions: they are all fairly consistent in indicating that work pressures tend to contribute to divisive rather than cohesive behaviors. The low pressure group clearly shows the most cohesive behavior and the least competitive behavior, and it contributes the major portion of the relationships thus far found. Moreover, it seems that high work pressure contributes to behaviors which might best be characterized as individually oriented, i.e., competitive.

In addition, when pressure is of short duration, there seems to be a slight tendency for a positive relationship between pressure and cohesive behavior, whereas when pressure is of long duration, there is a negative relationship between pressure and cohesive behavior. Apparently, the longer under pressure, the more individual behavior, as opposed to cooperative behavior, is rewarding.

Hypothesis 3: The Less Job Control People Have, the More the Cohesive Behavior

To test this hypothesis we used the index of job control. We divided our population into high and low job control groups and compared these groups on cohesive and competitive behavior. Since our main consideration was the conditioning effect of job control, comparisons were made within each pressure group in addition to the overall comparison. Hypotheses 4 and 5 were also tested in this manner. The results for Hypothesis 3 are illustrated in Figures 6 and 7.

These results are contrary to the hypothesis. In each pressure condition the more job control, the more the cohesive behavior. On an overall comparison groups with high

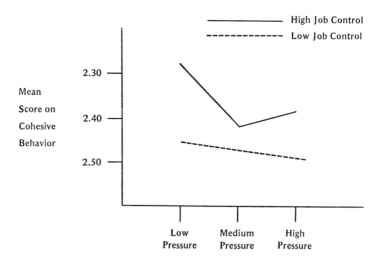

Figure 6
Relationship between Work Pressure and
Cohesive Behavior Controlling for Job Control
($\bar{X}$ Cohesive High Job Control − $\bar{X}$ Cohesive
Low Job Control P<.01)

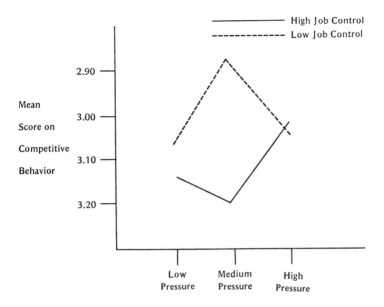

Figure 7
Relationship between Work Pressure and
Competitive Behavior Controlling for Job Control
($\overline{X}$ Competitive High Job Control – $\overline{X}$ Competitive
Low Job Control P<.01)

job control are significantly more cohesive than groups with low job control (P < .01). There is a slight tendency toward curvilinearity between pressure and cohesion when job control is high and toward a negative linearity when job control is low, but neither of these relationships is significant.

Job control also is associated with competitive behavior. The more job control, the less the competitive behavior, again contrary to our reasoning (P < .001). Moreover, the relationship between pressure and cohesion controlling for job control is unclear. In both cases there is curvilinearity, though neither relationship is significant. Under conditions of high pressure it makes little difference whether groups are high or low on job control with regard to competitive behavior.

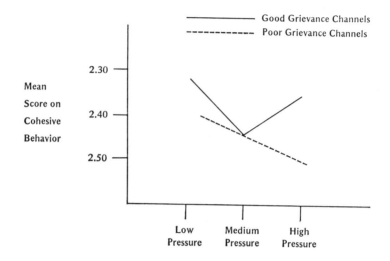

Figure 8
Relationship between Work Pressure and
Cohesive Behavior Controlling for Grievance Channels
($\overline{X}$ Cohesive Good Grievance Channels − $\overline{X}$ Cohesive
Poor Grievance Channels P<.02)

Hypothesis 4: The Less Effective the Grievance Channels, the More the Cohesive Behavior

Mean scores were computed for each department on our grievance channel index. An overall mean was computed and departments were divided into highs and lows on the basis of this mean. The results are illustrated in Figures 8 and 9.

Once again the results are in the direction opposite to the one hypothesized. Overall the more adequate the grievance channels, the more cohesive behavior (P < .02). Moreover, there is a clear negative relationship between pressure and group cohesion when grievance channels are poor, though this relationship is not significant. When grievance channels are adequate, there seems to be some tendency toward curvilinearity. The high pressure groups that have good grievance channels are almost as cohesive as the low pressure groups with good grievance channels.

Adequate grievance channels also relate to competitive

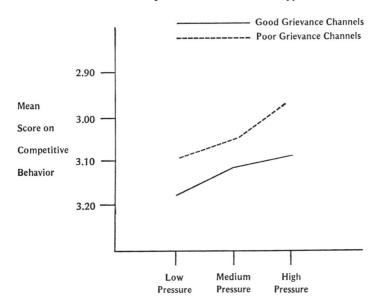

Figure 9
Relationship between Work Pressure and
Competitive Behavior Controlling for Grievance Channels
($\bar{X}$ Competitive Good Grievance Channels — $\bar{X}$ Competitive
Poor Grievance Channels P<.02)

behavior. The more the grievances are taken care of, the less the competitive behavior (P < .02). Moreover, the relationship between pressure and cohesive behavior is the same in both grievance channel conditions. In neither case is the relationship significant.

Hypothesis 5: The Less Stable the Standards, the More the Cohesive Behavior

A mean score was computed for the stable standards index. This was used as the dividing line between high and low stable standards groups. The results are illustrated in Figures 10 and 11.

Once again the results are opposite to the hypothesis. The more the standards are seen as moving, the less there seems to be cohesive behavior (P < .05). The relationship between pressure and cohesion under each of the conditions of stable standards is most interesting. Where standards are not stable, there is a negative and marginally significant relation (P < .10). The lower the pressure, the more the cohesion. Where the standards are stable, there is a distinct curvilinearity and this relationship is significant (P < .05).

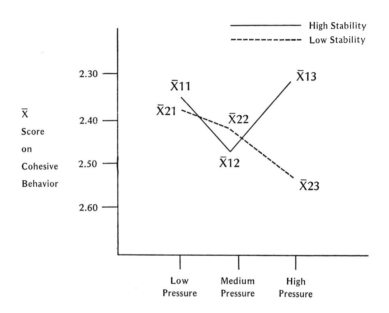

Figure 10
Relationship between Work Pressure and
Cohesive Behavior Controlling for Stability of Standards
(F X̄11, X̄12, X̄13 P<.05; P X̄21, X̄22, X̄23 F<.01;
X̄ Cohesive High Stability − X̄ Cohesive Low Stability P<.05)

Here we find that the group with the highest cohesive behavior is the high pressure group with stable standards. It doesn't seem to make much difference whether standards are stable or not in the other two groups. The facts that under conditions of high pressure and unstable standards the groups tend to be the least cohesive of all and that where standards are stable groups are the most cohesive are important findings which will be discussed further.

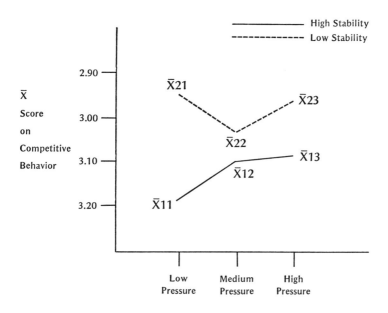

Figure 11
Relationship between Work Pressure and
Competitive Behavior Controlling for Stability of Standards
($\bar{X}11$-$\bar{X}22$ P<.05; $\bar{X}$ Competitive High Stability − $\bar{X}$ Competitive
Low Stability P<.01)

Stable standards are also related to competitive behavior. The more stable the standards, the less the competitive behavior $(P < .01)$.

Discussion

We can draw several conclusions from these data. The first is that the initial hypothesizing was wrong. We supposed that two things would happen under conditions of work pressure. First, we thought that employees would feel threatened by work pressures and would seek to alleviate this threat by becoming more cohesive and thus gaining mutual support and mutual cooperation. Moreover, we thought that social needs would be aroused which could be alleviated through cohesive behavior. Second, we believed that work pressures would take a significant portion of environmental control away from the operator and thereby motivate him to regain control through group action.

The first part of each of these statements is correct. As illustrated, work pressure seems to be threatening, and it is strongly associated with our measures of loss of environmental control. The problem is that neither threat nor loss of environmental control is positively associated with cohesive behavior. As we saw, the relationships between cohesive behavior and each of our measures of environmental control are negative and highly significant. Moreover, the fear index has a $-.08$ correlation with the cohesive index.

In conclusion, two things seem to be happening to the groups in this study. First, a reward structure has been set up by the company through its application of pressure that leads people to behave in an individually oriented manner rather than in a group-oriented manner. Pressure and its concomitants are strongly associated with competitive behavior and the absence of cohesive behaviors. Second, because the rewards are such that people do knuckle under and work faster and harder, there is less opportunity to "help one another," "stick up for one another," and otherwise engage in activities that are perceived as friendly. These two factors combined make cohesive responses quite untenable since there is neither time nor reward for these kinds of behaviors. Moreover, because people are motivated to work as fast as they can under strong pressure and unresponsive management, they perceive themselves "trying to work faster than each other," and this sets the stage for potential intragroup conflict. These findings will be explored in detail in the following chapter.

CHAPTER 5

Further Analysis
of the First Study

DESPITE OUR POOR RECORD in confirming hypotheses, our theory deserves further testing. We believed that under conditions of high work pressures and unresponsive management, the rewards for group action as a way of warding off the threat imposed by these conditions, regaining control over the environment, and satisfying social needs aroused by threat would be sufficiently great to offset the restrictions such group action might place on individual behavior. We failed, however, to anticipate correctly the reward structure in a nonunion industrial situation where management holds the trump cards. When management applies pressure, pressure must be met. Also, since employees are judged individually, they are also rewarded or punished individually: because they are strongly rewarded for individual behavior each employee works as fast as he can. This does not mean that group action or cohesive behavior must necessarily suffer. The fact that it does in this situation requires an explanation, which this chapter will provide.

We believed initially that the needs arising from work pressure, lack of job control, and unresponsive management[1] would be protective and control needs and that a good way for people to protect themselves and to regain environmental control might be to band together and present a solid front to management. However, another adaptive response would be to meet these pressures individually by doing exactly what the pressing agent wants, i.e., work as fast as possible.

This latter kind of response is similar to those described by Mintz (1951) and Hamblin (1958). In each of these cases, when no integrative behavior was obvious or available to members of a group or when they were rewarded for behaving individually and individual behavior was not consonant with cooperative behavior, then they behaved in an individually oriented way. These individually oriented behaviors tended to produce "conflict" within the group. This may be precisely what happened in our population.

Under high work pressure and unresponsive management the reward for working faster is the avoidance of threats from management. But while in a high pressure group the response of working faster is adaptive as a possible avenue for reducing the threat from management, it may be maladaptive from the viewpoint of cohesive behavior. In fact, it is a possible source of intragroup conflict because by definition productivity expectations are hard to meet in high pressure groups. Anyone who does meet or exceed them "proves" that this can be done and thereby casts aspersions on others in the group who have not yet come up to standards. Where pressure is low and/or management is responsive, there is less reason for people to behave competitively, and if competitive behavior does occur, it is not conflict-producing because it does not present a threat to others in the group. In our test situation almost everyone can meet the productivity requirements, and if someone tries to exceed them his action only conforms to the ethos built up in this company in the years preceding the pressure program.

On the basis of the foregoing knowledge we submit the following reasoning. The reward structure in the high pressure groups is such that people try to work as fast as they can. This is perceived rightly or wrongly as "trying to work faster than each other" (hereafter referred to as competitive be-

---

[1] Our concepts "grievance channels" and "stable standards" will hereafter be combined into an index called "responsive management." They are combined because they are highly correlated ($r = .57$) and because their operating characteristics in regard to our two major variables are virtually the same (see Chap. 3). We call the index responsive management because we believe that managers who do not adequately take care of complaints and who subject their workers to moving standards are unresponsive to the needs and wishes of their employees.

havior). In these groups the competitive act is the most threatening to individual members and consequently produces intragroup conflict, a condition not conducive to cohesive behavior.

In this study the reward structure is composed of three measurable elements. First are the work expectations themselves as measured by our pressure index; we have already found that there is more competitive behavior in the high pressure group. Second is the responsiveness of management in regard to reducing these pressures; if management is unresponsive, there should be a continual press for quantity and admonishments when the demand is not met. Third are the material rewards (i.e., higher pay) for increased production. If the last two elements occur more frequently under high pressure, then there should be even more incentive for competitive behavior. If in addition competitive behavior is most threatening under high pressure, its occurrence should produce a state of internal tension which will ramify into a lack of cohesive behavior. This reasoning will be tested in a series of hypotheses:[2]

A.   The more the work pressure, the more the rewards for working fast.

B.   The more the rewards for working fast, the more the competitive behavior.

C.   The more the work pressure, the more the dislike of competitive behavior.

D.   The more the work pressure, the more competitive behavior is negatively associated with cohesive behavior.

Testing the Hypotheses

Hypothesis A: The More the Work Pressure, the More the Rewards for Working Fast

To test this hypothesis, three operations were performed. The mean of our responsive management index was computed, and departments were divided into responsive and un-

[2] Obviously some of these hypotheses are post facto, but we believe that the data can best be developed by stating and then testing hypotheses.

responsive management groups on the basis of this mean. A mean was computed for the following item:

In recommending one of his employees for a *salary increase,* how important does your manager consider the employee's doing a large amount of work? (We know that you cannot be certain about this, but we would like your best guess). CHECK ONE:
1. Very important
2. Quite important
3. Somewhat important
4. Not too important
5. Not at all important

The departments were then divided into high pay for quantity and low pay for quantity groups on the basis of this mean. The percentage of departments within each pressure group that attained the rewarding conditions for working fast was then computed. The results, which support Hypothesis A, are shown in Table 4.

TABLE 4

PERCENTAGE OF GROUPS THAT ATTAINED TWO REWARDING CONDITIONS FOR WORKING FAST, BY PRESSURE CONDITION

Rewarding Condition	Low Pressure	Medium Pres-sure	High Pres-sure	X^2	P 2df
Unresponsive manage-ment	18%	50%	66%	24.20	<.01
High pay for quantity of work	36%	54%	68%	10.35	<.01

Hypothesis B: The More the Rewards for Working Fast, the More Competitive Behavior

To test this hypothesis the mean scores on competitive behavior were computed for the responsive and unresponsive management groups and for the high pay for quantity and low pay for quantity groups. The differences in competitive behavior were then compared. The results are presented in Table 5.

Hypothesis B is thus confirmed. Those groups which are subjected to unresponsive management or to high pay for quantity of work are significantly more competitive.

TABLE 5

MEAN SCORES ON COMPETITIVE BEHAVIOR WITHIN
TWO CONDITIONS OF REWARD FOR WORKING FAST

Rewarding Condition	Mean Competitive Behavior Score*	S.D. of Difference	P within each Rewarding Condition
Responsive management	3.12		
Unresponsive management	3.00	.052	<.05
Low pay for quantity of work	3.18		
High pay for quantity of work	2.96	.048	<.001

* The lower the score, the more the competitive behavior.

Hypothesis C: The More the Work Pressure, the More Competitive Behavior Is Disliked by Group Members

To test this hypothesis mean scores on the following item were computed for each pressure group. The results are presented in Table 6.

How much do the people in your department dislike an employee who tries to work a lot faster than the others?
CHECK ONE:
1. They dislike him very much
2. They dislike him quite a bit
3. They dislike him somewhat
4. They dislike him a little
5. They do not dislike him at all

TABLE 6

MEAN SCORE ON DISLIKE OF
COMPETITIVE BEHAVIOR FOR EACH PRESSURE GROUP

Pressure Condition	Mean Score on Dislike of Competitive Behavior	F	P
Low pressure	3.46		
Medium pressure	3.24	6.39	<.01
High pressure	3.07		

Hypothesis D: The More the Work Pressure, the More Competitive Behavior Is Negatively Associated with Cohesive Behavior

This hypothesis was tested by breaking the groups into high and low competitive behavior groups within pressure groups. The mean score on cohesive behavior was then computed for each of these groups and the scores were compared. The results are shown in Figure 12.

The results support the hypothesis. Under low and medium pressure there is no relationship between competitive behavior and cohesive behavior, but under high pressure there is a significant negative relationship (P < .05). When high pressure groups are not competitive, they have about as much cohesive behavior as low pressure groups. Note, too, that when we control for competitive behavior, a significant negative relationship between pressure and cohesive behavior remains under high competition since P < .05.

All the new hypotheses are supported by the evidence. We can conclude then that one of the things contributing to the lack of cohesive behavior in the high pressure groups is that the kinds of behaviors for which individuals are rewarded in these groups are internally threatening to the groups. Since the rewards provide powerful incentives, many people behave competitively despite the group sanctions, producing intragroup conflict which is negatively associated with group cohesion. Let us pursue this reasoning.

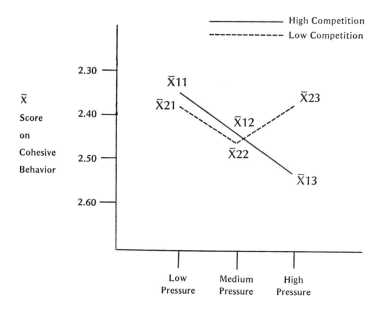

Figure 12
Relationship between Work Pressure and
Cohesive Behavior Controlling for Competitive Behavior
(F $\bar{X}11$, $\bar{X}12$, $\bar{X}13$ P<.05; t $\bar{X}13$, 23 P<.05)

Since our index of responsive management comprises the stable standards and grievance channel indices, we would expect unresponsive management to provide a setting in which competitive behavior is threatening, much as high pressure does. For instance, our moving standards items measure the extent to which an increased amount of work results in management expecting still more both from the individual employee and from the group. Moreover, if others in the group meet "unfair" work expectations, the definition of "unfairness" for that group changes, and a grievance in regard to "unfair" work expectations becomes an unwarranted complaint. Thus in these kinds of groups the employee who tries to work faster than the rest places the other members in jeopardy. Following this reasoning, we make the following hypotheses:

E. The more unresponsive the management, the more people dislike competitive behavior.

F. Under conditions of unresponsive management and high pressure there will be the most dislike of competitive behavior.

G. Under conditions of unresponsive management and high pressure there will be the most competitive behavior.

H. When people compete under conditions of unresponsive management and high pressure, there will be the least cohesive behavior of any group.

Hypothesis E: The More Unresponsive the Management, the More People Dislike Competitive Behavior

To test this hypothesis we broke the groups into responsive and unresponsive management groups on the basis of the mean for that index. Then we compared the mean scores of these groups on our measure of dislike of competitive behavior. The mean score for the responsive management group is 3.44, whereas the mean score for the unresponsive management group is 3.04. The difference is highly significant (P < .001) and in the direction hypothesized—the lower the score, the more the dislike.

Hypothesis F: Under Conditions of Unresponsive Management and High Pressure There Will Be the Most Dislike of Competitive Behavior

To test this hypothesis we compared the mean scores of responsive and unresponsive management groups on dislike of competitive behavior. For clarity of reporting and since no group approached the high pressure–unresponsive management group in amount of dislike of competitive behavior, the medium and low pressure groups were combined. The results are presented in Figure 13.

It is clear that the most dislike of competitive behavior occurs under high pressure and unresponsive management together, as hypothesized.

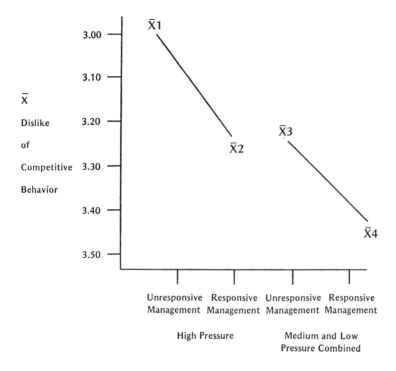

Figure 13
Relationship between Responsive Management and
Dislike of Competitive Behavior under
Two Conditions of Work Pressure
(t $\bar{X}1$, $\bar{X}3$ P<.02; t $\bar{X}1$, $\bar{X}4$ P<.001)

Hypothesis G: Under Conditions of Unresponsive Management and High Pressure There Will Be the Most Competitive Behavior

This hypothesis was tested in the same way by comparing the same groups on their mean scores for competitive behavior. The results are presented in Figure 14.

Again the hypothesis is confirmed. The high pressure–unresponsive management group has the most competitive behavior. It is significantly different from two of the other groups shown. The medium and low pressure–unresponsive management group has less competitive behavior than the

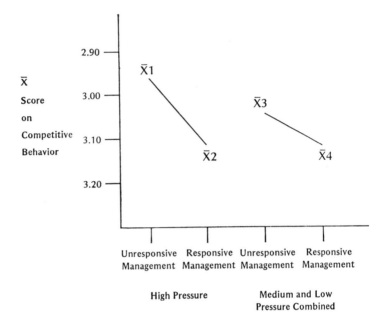

Figure 14
Relationship between Responsive Management and
Competitive Behavior under Two Conditions of
Work Pressure (t $\bar{X}1$, $\bar{X}2$ P<.05; t $\bar{X}1$, $\bar{X}4$ P<.02)

high pressure–unresponsive management group, though not significantly so. Moreover, it is the second highest group on competitive behavior. Although it is not shown, this result also illustrates that high pressure and unresponsive management have somewhat independent effects on competitive behavior.

Hypothesis H: When People Compete under Conditions of Severe Management and High Pressure, There Will Be the Least Cohesive Behavior

To test this hypothesis we compared the high competitive groups with the low competitive groups under conditions of high pressure and responsive and unresponsive management. In no case did any of the groups under medium and low pressure approach the high pressure–unresponsive management group, which was highly competitive, in regard to amount of cohesive behavior. Consequently they were combined. The results of the comparison are presented in Figure 15.

The high pressure–unresponsive management group that is also highly competitive clearly has the least cohesive behavior. It is significantly different from all other groups. It is interesting to note that while unresponsive management

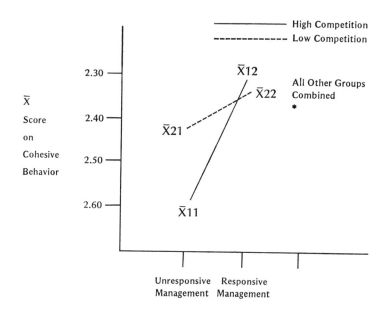

Figure 15
Relationship between Responsive Management and
Cohesive Behavior under High Work Pressure
(t $\bar{X}11$, $\bar{X}12$, P<.001; t $\bar{X}11$, $\bar{X}21$ P<.01; t $\bar{X}11$, $\bar{X}22$ P<.01)

may have some small independent effect on cohesive behavior, competitive behavior has none. Competitive behavior has to occur under special conditions in order to be negatively associated with cohesive behavior. Another interesting point is that the high pressure–responsive management condition is associated with high cohesive behavior. This suggests that there is something managers can do even under high pressure to make cohesive responses tenable. We will deal with this in Chapter 6.

In sum, Hypotheses A–H are all supported by the data. Specifically, high pressure together with unresponsive management produces the most competitive behavior, the most dislike of competitive behavior, and the least cohesive behavior.

Other Aspects of the Reward Structure

Other aspects of the pertinent reward structure have not yet been discussed. For instance, managers can reward employees for helping others in the department. If members of a group are well rewarded for cooperation, it is plausible to predict that there will be more cohesive behavior. We also made an assumption based on our review of the cohesion literature that cohesive behavior should be rewarding in its own right. If this is so, then one of the reasons for the lack of cohesive behavior in our study might be that it is prevented. A number of conditions might prevent cohesive behavior, one of which might be the lack of personal control over behavior. Earlier we dealt with this when we showed that there was less job control in the high pressure groups than in the other groups. Another aspect of personal control might simply be the availability of time to engage in cohesive behaviors.

Two items in the questionnaire measured the extent to which cooperative behaviors are rewarded and the amount of time available for them:

In recommending one of his employees for a *salary increase,* how important does your manager consider the employee's helping out other employees in the department? (We know that you cannot be certain about this, but we would like your best guess.) CHECK ONE:
1. Extremely important
2. Quite important
3. Somewhat important
4. Not at all important

Employees sometimes stop their work and have a cup of coffee, chat with their friends, or relax in other ways. About how much time can you take each day to relax these ways?

CHECK ONE:

1. No time at all
2. One to two minutes
3. Three to five minutes
4. Five to ten minutes
5. Ten to twenty minutes
6. More than twenty minutes

We computed the mean for each of these items and the percentage of each pressure group that scored high on each item. The results are shown in Table 7.

TABLE 7

PERCENTAGE OF EACH PRESSURE GROUP THAT SCORED
HIGH ON REWARDS FOR COOPERATION AND
TIME AVAILABLE FOR COHESIVE BEHAVIOR

	Low Pressure	Medium Pressure	High Pressure	X^2	P
Rewards for cooperation	60%	48%	34%	6.95	<.05
Time available for cohesive behavior	70%	46%	26%	19.49	<.01

These results suggest strong negative relationships between pressure and rewards for cooperation and between pressure and time for cohesive behavior.

To see if these variables affect cohesive behavior, we broke the groups into high and low groups within each variable and compared their mean scores on cohesive behavior. The results are presented in Table 8.

The difference in cohesive behavior is small in both cases, but in the predicted direction. We must conclude therefore that these variables themselves have a marginal effect on cohesive behavior. In Chapter 6 we will explore the possibility

TABLE 8

COMPARISON OF MEAN SCORES ON COHESIVE BEHAVIOR
FOR REWARDS FOR COOPERATION AND TIME FOR
COHESIVE BEHAVIOR

Mean Score on Cohesive Behavior*		S.D. $\overline{X}$	S.D.$\overline{X}$1–$\overline{X}$2	P
Rewards for cooperation	High	2.39	.0371	N.S.
	Low	2.44		
Time for cohesive behavior	High	2.38	.0401	.05
	Low	2.46		

* The higher the score, the less the cohesive behavior.

that reward for cooperation has a conditioning effect on the relationship between pressure and cohesive behavior.

Discussion

We have seen that the reward structure in the high pressure groups is clearly conducive to competitive behavior. In these groups there is more incentive to try to work as fast as possible because there is a greater discrepancy between the productivity expectations of management and the actual level of productivity. Moreover, there is a strong tendency for management to be unremitting in regard to these expectations. Grievances about too much work are less likely to be heard sympathetically, there are more moving standards, and there is more emphasis on quantity of work as a criterion for a salary increase.

These factors add up to a powerful incentive for the individual employee to work as fast as he can (behave competitively), and in the high pressure groups, where quantity of work is extremely important and a large percentage of employees feel that they are not measuring up to productivity expectations, competitive behavior constitutes an intragroup threat. Furthermore, the presence of competitive behavior is associated with a lack of cohesive behavior. In groups where the quantity of work is not as important, competitive behavior presents no intragroup threat and consequently is not associated with cohesive behavior in any way.

The data are open to another interpretation that is not altogether contradictory to the one above. Perhaps the reason groups which do not compete under high pressure show high cohesive behavior is that they are cohesive to begin with and effectively stifle the threatening competitive behavior—that is, that they do not compete because they are cohesive, not that they are cohesive because they do not compete. There is probably some truth to this idea of causality, but because we do not have an adequate "before" measure of cohesiveness we will never know the extent of its truth. However, the data support the first interpretation of the results as the major explanation of the dynamics for three reasons.

First, the "time" data (Figures 4 and 5) support our reasoning. We found that the longer groups were under pressure, the more there was a tendency to compete within the group and that under conditions of high pressure there was less cohesive behavior. There is no reason to believe that the groups earlier subjected to the reward structure of high pressure were any less cohesive than those later subjected to pressure.[3] It would seem, then, that the longer groups are subjected to the reward structure characteristic of our high pressure situation, the greater the tendency to respond to these pressures by competing.

Second, if the high pressure–low competition groups were highly cohesive before pressure was introduced, we would expect them to show up as extremely cohesive considering the new pressures with which they are faced. However, the forces which produce competitive behavior are the strongest in these groups, and it would require an equally strong counterforce, such as very high group cohesion, to suppress the competitive response effectively. This counterforce is

[3] The new standards program was introduced on the basis of industrial engineering criteria such as measurability of output. There is no relationship between measurability of output or its correlates, skill level and job variability, with cohesive behavior when pressure is used as a control variable.

not present, as Figure 12 illustrates. The high pressure–low competition groups, while high on cohesive behavior, are still no higher than the low pressure groups as a whole. We would expect the highest cohesive groups to be those which do not compete in the face of high work pressure and unresponsive management, but Figure 15 illustrates that this is not true since the noncompetitive group is not as cohesive as the groups that have responsive management under high pressure.

Third, the fact that under high pressure there is the least cohesive behavior and under low pressure the most cannot be explained by stating that the reason for low competition under high pressure is high group cohesion before the introduction of pressure.

Taken together, these three factors suggest that our first interpretation is the best explanation of the total dynamics of the situation. Thus, while we cannot reject the possibility that the initially cohesive nature of the noncompetitive high pressure groups produces the differences in cohesive behavior, the evidence suggests that what happens after pressure is applied really makes the difference, and this is determined more by the balance of rewards and costs than by the initial characteristics of the group.

We also find that in the low pressure groups quite a different reward structure exists from that of the high pressure groups. Management does not push, either in a punitive manner or by paying for quantity of production. Also there is a significantly greater emphasis on rewarding co-operative behavior, though this latter factor is only marginally related to cohesive behavior. Finally, low pressure groups have a great deal more time to devote to cohesive behavior. If we accept the assumption that cohesive behavior as measured in the study has its own rewards, then the opportunity to behave cohesively should be associated with actual behavior. This is what we find. Thus we must conclude that in the low pressure groups there is less intragroup conflict potential because quantity of production is not an issue and because individual behaviors in regard to quantity of production present less threat than in the high pressure groups. In addition because of the reward structure, which includes a relatively high reward for cooperative behavior and the opportunity to engage in potentially rewarding cohesive activities such as being friendly or helping others on the job, there is somewhat more cohesive behavior.

Summary

Some major conclusions emerged from the further analysis of the data from the first study. Under high pressure the reward structure provides a powerful incentive for competitive behavior, and as a result more competitive behavior occurs. However, there are strong group sanctions against competitive behavior in the high pressure groups. Therefore, when competitive behavior occurs under high pressure, there is likely to be high intragroup conflict which is not consonant with cohesive behavior. We suggested that these three factors provide a reasonable explanation of why there is low cohesive behavior under high work pressure. Also we found that there were somewhat more rewards for cooperation and more time available for cohesive behavior in the low pressure group.

CHAPTER 6

Replication of the First Study

A REPLICATION of the first study was performed on an entirely different industrial population. The methods used in gathering the data were precisely the same. While there was only about a 50 percent overlap in the two questionnaires, the items used in the replication were precisely those used in the first study, with two exceptions, which will be discussed later.

In addition to the replication we will extend the investigation to test an important lead developed in the first study. One of our major conclusions was that competition within a group under conditions of high pressure produces intragroup conflict, which is not consonant with cohesive behavior. The second study provides us with an opportunity specifically to test this reasoning.

Comparison of First and Second Study Populations on Important Variables

The two test populations were similar: they were composed of production workers grouped in departments of similar size, they received identical company benefits, they were not unionized, and they reported identical amounts of work pressure as measured by two items asking them in different ways how they felt about the amount of work expected of them. In each population an average of 23 percent responded "too much." However, the two populations also differed in four important respects.

The first population was on the average a more highly

skilled population. Moreover, it had more varied skills with a range from highly routine, repetitive tasks to highly skilled, long-cycle tasks. Sixty-five of the 172 departments in the total population were classified as having repetitive, short-cycle jobs. In the second population 59 of the 112 departments were so classified, with the rest being more highly skilled.

Despite the fact that the populations had identical feelings of work pressure, the meaning of pressure to individual employees may have been different in the two groups. In the first population the notion of a fair day's work for a fair day's pay was traditionally connected with laissez faire management. When pressure was finally introduced into this population, it was virtually all at once, with rather severe productivity demands being made on a sizable portion of the population. The second population had a tradition of high work pressure and a production setup geared to a fairly fast pace. Pressure had been increasing over the years; it did not come suddenly as in the first population. The two populations were considered by the corporate manufacturing management to be at approximately the same level of productivity at the time of the second study. Thus before the new standards program the first population had been at a lower productivity level than the second population.

The first population generally indicated a lower absolute level of cohesive behavior than the second as measured by our three cohesive behavior items. However, there was more competitive behavior in the second population. It is impossible to assess the reasons for these differences.

The first population was largely of northern or western origin. Most of the population was industrially sophisticated in the sense of having been in and around other industries. This was not true of the second population, which was derived mostly from a border state and whose surrounding area has few other industries. These differences must be kept in mind. However, as we shall see, they don't seem to make much difference in terms of the relationships among variables.

Difference in the Measurement of the Independent Variable

We mentioned that there was a rather distinct difference in the way pressure was applied in each of these populations. In the first study pressure came at a designated point in time. Virtually everybody in the population was subjected to the pressure and could state specifically when the pressure was introduced and whether or not he was able to meet it in terms of his productivity.

In the second population, pressure was a constant and virtually everybody could meet the demand, though with varying degrees of ease. Consequently our pressure index for the first study (i.e., the percentage of people who were asked to increase their productivity and could not do it) seemed inappropriate for the second study population,[1] and a measure had to be found which closely approximated the independent variable of the first study.

We found two things to be true of our pressure variables in the first study which helped us substantially to overcome our dilemma. First, we ran a correlation between a subjective pressure index of our first study and our objective pressure index and obtained a coefficient of .74. This was sufficiently high to assume that in large part these two indices were measuring the same thing. Second, we ran a correlation between each of these indices and cohesive behavior. The correlations were identical: −.22 in each case. Thus not only were the two indices highly related, but they also related similarly to our dependent variable.

As a result, though it was not as satisfactory as an identical index to the one in the first study, we decided to use a subjective index of pressure in the second study as our independent variable. It was composed of four well-correlated items:

[1] In checking this assumption against the data we found that indeed there was little variability in the second population on the objective index. Very few departments had more than 10 percent who said they were asked to increase production but could not do it. Thus there was really no independent variable according to our objective index. However, according to the subjective index the distribution of people saying "too much" work was about the same.

How do you feel about the amount of work you are expected to do?
1. Too much
2. About the right amount
3. I would prefer to do more

How do you think most of the people you work with feel about the amount of work they are expected to do?
1. Most of them feel that they are expected to do too much
2. Most of them feel that they are expected to do about the right amount
3. Most of them would prefer to do more

Is it difficult for you to turn out the amount of work expected of you?
1. No, not at all difficult for me to do this
2. Yes, a little difficult
3. Yes, fairly difficult
4. Yes, quite difficult
5. Yes, it is very difficult for me to do this

On the job, do you feel any pressure for increasing your production *above* what you yourself think is reasonable?
1. Yes, I feel a great deal of pressure to do this
2. Yes, considerable pressure
3. Yes, a little pressure
4. I feel no pressure at all to do this

The lowest correlation among these items is .51. Moreover, as an index, they correlate .64 with the item "Have you been asked to increase the amount of work you do over the past two years?" Thus we believed that the four questions were a good enough representation of "objective" pressure to approximate closely the index used in the first study.

Another item which was somewhat different in the second study was our measure of the extent to which people dislike others who compete. The item was changed from:

How much do the people in your department dislike an employee who tries to work a lot faster than the others?
1. They dislike him very much

2. They dislike him quite a bit
3. They dislike him somewhat
4. They dislike him a little
5. They do not dislike him at all

to:

If someone in your department turned out a great deal more work than the other employees, would this help or hurt his getting along with them?

Hurt very much				Neither help nor hurt				Help very much		
0	1	2	3	4	5	6	7	8	9	10

The item was changed for reasons not pertinent to the subject of this study. As we shall see, the change may make a difference in one of our relationships, but it has no bearing whatsoever on our main findings.

Two new variables extended the previous study. The first, designed to tap intragroup conflict, consisted of the following items:[2]

How many people in your department do the following things?
1. Try to get ahead at the expense of others
2. Blame others when there is trouble getting the work out

The alternatives for each of these items were identical to the alternatives for the cohesiveness items and the competitive item of the first study.

The second new variable was the extent to which managers applied pressure on a group basis. That is, did the manager exhort the group to perform better as a group in addition to or instead of exhorting individual employees to work as fast as they could? To measure this variable we used the following item:

---

[2] We included four other cohesiveness items in this new study, but we will not deal with these in our replication or extension. Because they correlate highly with the cohesiveness behavior index but hardly at all with the competitive item in the first study, we believed that including them in the new cohesive behavior index would only complicate matters and not add anything in terms of results. Therefore we included only the variables which served the replication and extension.

How often does your manager encourage your department to do better work than other departments?

Always   Never

| 0 | 1 | 2 | 3 | 4 | 5 | 6 | 7 | 8 | 9 | 10 |

The first study resulted in four major findings. First, cohesiveness is a multidimensional concept including behaviors which may or may not be related and which can relate to other variables in different ways. Significantly, competitive behavior and social-supportive (cohesive) behavior are not related directly. Second, there is a small though significant negative relationship between work pressure and cohesive behavior. Moreover, there is a small and marginally significant positive relationship between work pressure and competitive behavior. Third, the reward structure in the high pressure situation leads people to compete, and in conditions of high pressure competitive behavior is threatening to members of groups. This is one of the reasons that less cohesive behavior results under conditions of high pressure. When people do not compete in the high pressure groups, there is relatively high cohesive behavior. Fourth, the reward structure in the low pressure situation is conducive to cohesive behavior, though it seems to have only marginal effects. Each of these findings was tested in the new study. In addition a major assertion upon which our reasoning rests, that under high pressure competitive behavior produces intragroup conflict which is not consonant with cohesive behavior, was directly tested with our new group conflict items.

We made more effective use of the correlation coefficient in the second study because, unlike the first study, all the groups available for analysis were used, and there was no arbitrary buffer zone between pressure groups. Thus our major independent variable was continuous and consequently amenable to correlational analysis. When interactive effects were hypothesized, as in controlling for competitive behavior or unresponsive management, we used tests for the significance of difference in mean scores.

Our population consisted of ninety-three production departments which were selected according to the same criteria used in the first study, i.e., the departments had to be engaged in production work and there had to be at least six people in each group. There were 1,356 employees involved.

The second study will be analyzed in this fashion: first, we will look at the correlation matrix and the factor analysis to see if social-supportive and competitive behaviors emerged as they did in the first study. Second, we will examine the relationships among variables in replication of the findings of the first study. Third, we will test the effects of pressure on intragroup conflict.

Dimensions of Group Behavior

Tables 9 and 10 show that the results of the second study are virtually the same as those of the first study. The cohesive behavior items are well correlated with one another as before

TABLE 9

CORRELATION MATRIX OF GROUP
BEHAVIORS USING PEARSON'S r^*

How many people in your department	A	B	C	D	E	F
A. Stick up for one another?		.60	49	−23	−48	−46
B. Help one another on the job?			57	−20	−36	−39
C. Are friendly to one another?				−20	−47	−47
D. Try to work faster than each other?					40	35
E. Try to get ahead at the expense of each other?						.70
F. Blame each other when there is trouble getting the work out?						

* Groups were the unit of analysis.

TABLE 10

FACTOR ANALYSIS OF GROUP BEHAVIOR ITEMS*

How many people in your department	1 Cohesive factor	2 Intragroup conflict factor	3
A. Stick up for one another?	.74	−.02	0
B. Help one another on the job?	.79	−.09	.01
C. Are friendly to one another?	.70	−.27	.02
D. Try to work faster than each other?	−.19	.29	.26
E. Try to get ahead at the expense of each other?	−.31	.49	.13
F. Blame each other when there is trouble getting the work out?	−.23	.66	.10

* Groups were the unit of analysis.

but are not well correlated with the competitive item. Moreover, the factor analysis indicates a strong contingency among the cohesive behavior items but little contingency between the cohesive items and the competitive item.

The new items designed to measure intragroup conflict correlate moderately well with both the cohesiveness and the competitiveness items and quite well with each other. On the factor analysis they emerge as a separate factor, though the competition item has its first-order loading on this factor. It is quite small, however, and not well differentiated. Therefore it can be considered to have only marginal contingency with the intragroup conflict items. While this result is not as clear-cut as we would like, it shows that competitive behavior and intragroup conflict behavior are not necessarily of the same order. Therefore we can use the competitive item as a control, as we did in the first study.

Work Pressure Is Negatively Associated with Cohesive Behavior and Positively Associated with Competitive Behavior

Figures 16 and 17 show a clear replication of the results in the first study. There is a small though highly significant negative correlation between work pressure and group cohesive behavior. Moreover, there is a fairly strong positive relationship between work pressure and competitive behavior —a much clearer relationship than in the first study.

The Reward Structure as a Consequence of Work Pressure

The effects of work pressure on the reward structure are clear and unambiguous. In all cases the rewards are conducive to competitive behavior and antithetical to cohesive behavior (see Table 11). Also, each of the variables that is likely to produce competition in fact seems to do so (see Table 12).

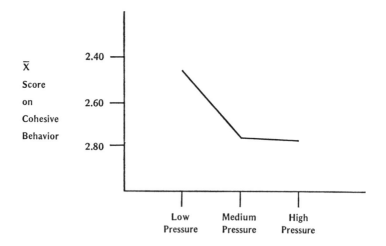

Figure 16
Relationship between Work Pressure and
Cohesive Behavior, Second Study (r =-.25, P<.02)*

*See Appendix A for a methodological note on the scale
for all variables in the second study.

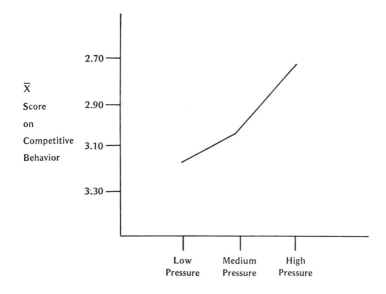

Figure 17
Relationship between Work Pressure and
Competitive Behavior, Second Study (r =.41, P<.001)

TABLE 11

RELATIONSHIP BETWEEN WORK PRESSURE AND
VARIOUS ASPECTS OF THE REWARD STRUCTURE

Correlation between pressure and	r	P
Unresponsive management	.63	.001
Quantity of work as a criterion for pay increase	.57	.001
Supervisory encouragement of competition*	.47	.001
Helping others as a criterion for pay increase	−.33	.01
Supervisory encouragement of cooperation*	−.19	N.S.

* New items in second study

TABLE 12

RELATIONSHIPS BETWEEN ASPECTS OF THE
REWARD STRUCTURE AND GROUP BEHAVIORS
THEY ARE EXPECTED TO PRODUCE

	r	P
Correlation between competitiveness and		
Unresponsive management	.31	.01
Quantity of work as a criterion		
for salary increase	.44	.001
Supervisory encouragement of		
competition	.32	.01
Correlation between cohesiveness and		
Helping others as a criterion		
for salary increase	.15	N.S.
Supervisory encouragement		
of cooperation	.17	N.S.

The results are less clear concerning the effects of the reward structure on cohesive behavior. While in the low pressure condition there seems to be more reward for cohesive behavior, these rewards are not highly associated with the cohesive acts themselves. The fact that all the results replicate the first study, however, enables us to conclude with some confidence that high pressure is conducive to competitive behavior but not to cohesive behavior.

Dislike of Competitive Behavior under Conditions of High Pressure

In the first study we found that both pressure and unresponsive management were positively related to a dislike of competitive behavior.[3] The results of the second study are shown in Table 13. We see that while the correlation between pressure and dislike of people who work fast produces a P equal to .05, it is quite small, explaining only 4 percent of the total variance. Moreover, it is not nearly as significant as in

---

[3] Recall that our measure of dislike of competitive behavior was not the same in the two studies. In the first study we explicitly asked, "How much do the people in your department dislike an employee who tries to work faster than the others?" In the second study we asked, "If someone turned out a great deal more work than the others, would this help or hurt his getting along?"

TABLE 13

RELATIONSHIP BETWEEN DISLIKE OF COMPETITIVE
BEHAVIOR AND CONDITIONS LIKELY TO PRODUCE
COMPETITIVE BEHAVIOR

Correlation between dislike of competition and	*r*	P
Pressure	.20	.05
Unresponsive management	.06	N.S.

the first study, where we obtained a P of .01. In this study we would need a correlation of at least .27 to produce a comparable level of significance, and such a correlation would explain almost twice as much of the variance as the correlation we obtained. Nevertheless, because the new result replicates the previous findings, we conclude that pressure is positively correlated with a dislike of people who compete.

There is no relationship between unresponsive management and dislike of competition, a finding quite unlike the findings of the first study. Perhaps the difference between the two populations on this variable resides in the fact that our measure of dislike of competition was different. Unfortunately, there is no way of testing this, though the finding underlines the need for replication studies using different populations.

The Higher the Work Pressure, the More Competition Is Negatively Associated with Cohesive Behavior

As Figure 18 illustrates, this finding of the first study is replicated. In terms of the hypothesis in the second study the relationships are actually better in that competition becomes more negatively associated with cohesion as we move from low to high pressure, even though the level of significance of the difference between the high and low competitive groups under high pressure is not large. The fact that a replication occurs, however, is in our estimation more impressive than the absolute level of significance. We conclude, therefore, that under low pressure there is little or no difference in co-

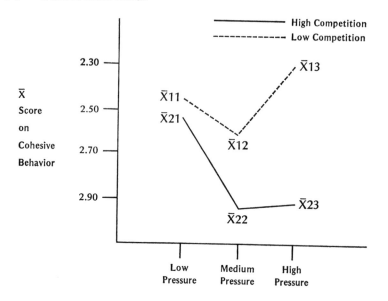

Figure 18
Relationship between Work Pressure and
Cohesive Behavior Controlling for Competitive Behavior,
Second Study (t $\bar{X}$13, $\bar{X}$23 P<.10)

hesiveness between the high and the low competitive groups but that under high pressure there is a definite negative relationship between competitiveness and cohesiveness, as illustrated in both studies.

Three other findings presented in Chapter 4 supported in some detail our major line of reasoning. First, we found the most competitive behavior under conditions of high pressure where management was unresponsive. This finding was replicated in the second study. The mean score of the high pressure–unresponsive management group on the competitive item was 2.66, whereas the next highest competition group had a mean of 2.86 (the lower the score, the more the competition).[4]

---

[4] The difference between these two groups is not significant. However, taking the high pressure–unresponsive management group against all other conditions combined ($\bar{X} = 3.05$), the difference is significant at the .05 level.

Second, we found the most dislike of competition in the high pressure–unresponsive management group, a situation which we hypothesized would lead to the greatest intragroup conflict and consequently the lowest cohesion. In the second study this hypothesis was not supported. The most dislike of competition occurred in the middle pressure–unresponsive management group, with the high pressure–unresponsive management group falling somewhere in the middle. This finding may be a consequence of the different measure of dislike of competition in the second study.[5]

Third, we found the least cohesive behavior in the high pressure–unresponsive management groups that were high in competitive behavior. This finding was replicated in the second study. The mean cohesiveness score for this group was 2.95, with the second lowest group having a mean score of 2.88.[6] Moreover, in looking at the high pressure groups only, we find a virtual duplication in the two studies. The combination of high pressure–unresponsive management and competitive behavior is associated with the least cohesive behavior, as Figure 19 shows. The other combinations do not seem to matter much in terms of cohesive behavior.

Extension of the First Study

We hypothesized that the reason for the low cohesiveness in the high pressure group was that the situation held the most intragroup conflict potential.[7] The employees were rewarded for competing and did compete even though there

[5] This finding would seem to be a weak link in our chain of reasoning since we believed that the low cohesion under high pressure was due in part to the high propensity for competitive behavior along with the most dislike of competitive behavior which would create intragroup conflict. However, as we shall see in our discussion of the extension, the highest intragroup conflict does occur as hypothesized in the high pressure group—specifically in high pressure–unresponsive management groups that compete.

[6] This difference is not statistically significant. However, comparing the high pressure–unresponsive management group that was also highly competitive against all the other groups combined ($\bar{X} = 2.55$), we obtain a difference that is significant at the .05 level.

[7] In testing the relationship between work pressure and intragroup conflict, we find a correlation of .33 and a significance level $> .01$. This supports the thesis that work pressure is associated with intragroup conflict.

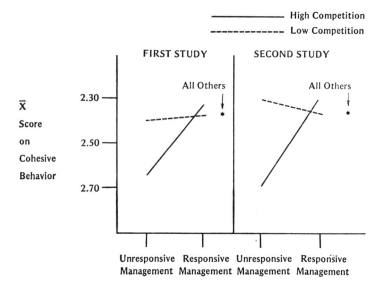

HIGH PRESSURE ONLY

Figure 19
Comparison of the Two Study Populations in Regard to the
Combined Effects of Unresponsive Management, High Work Pressure,
and High Competitive Behavior on Cohesive Behavior
(Scale is not exact for second study but approximation is good.)

were strong group sanctions against this behavior. We believed that this competition would produce intragroup conflict. To test this reasoning we formed an index of the intragroup conflict items previously described. Using this index,
we found the relationship between pressure and intragroup
conflict controlling for competitive behavior, as shown in
Figure 20.

These results support our hypothesis. The greatest difference between high competitive and low competitive groups
in terms of group conflict occurs in the high pressure condition, though the difference in the medium pressure condition is also significant. In the low pressure groups there is
no relationship at all between competitive behavior and
intragroup conflict. Thus the relationship between pressure
and intragroup conflict controlling for competitive behavior

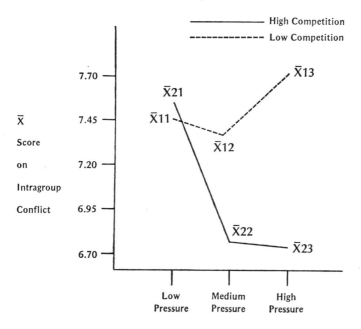

Figure 20
Relationship between Work Pressure and Intragroup
Conflict Controlling for Competitive Behavior
(t $\bar{X}12$, $\bar{X}22$ P<.05; t $\bar{X}13$, $\bar{X}23$ P<.02)

is almost identical to the relationship between pressure and cohesive behavior using the same control, even though cohesive behavior and intragroup conflict behavior emerge as fairly distinct factors on our factor analysis.

Discussion and Conclusions

Most of the results of the first study are replicated in the second study despite some major differences between the populations. Different classes of behavior occur within a group and emerge as separate factors on a factor analysis even though there are moderately high correlations among them. Moreover, as demonstrated in both studies, at least two of these classes have different relationships to one another under different environmental conditions. Under low pres-

sure competitive behavior has no relationship to cohesive behavior, whereas under high pressure there is a significant
negative relationship. In addition, as demonstrated in the
second study, there is a similar effect with regard to the relationship between competitive behavior and intragroup
conflict. When pressure is low, there is no association between competitive behavior and intragroup conflict, whereas
when pressure is high, there is a strong positive association.

We also found that the negative relationship between cohesive behavior and work pressure and the positive relationship between competitive behavior and work pressure
obtained in both studies. The dynamics seem to be the same
in both populations. Rewards from management for competitive behavior are strongest in high pressure situations
and are strongly associated with the actual occurrence of
competitive behavior. We reasoned that competitive behavior would be most threatening to persons under high pressure and that if it occurred, it would lead to intragroup
conflict, a situation not consonant with cohesive behavior. In
the main this reasoning was supported in both studies. We
also suggested that an extreme example of this reasoning
would occur in groups under high pressure and unresponsive
management. In both studies we found the most competition
under this condition and hence the most intragroup conflict
and the least cohesive behavior.

All these results imply a causal chain. First, work pressure
occurs. This and all it embodies (i.e., emphasis on quantity
of work, unresponsive management, and rewards encouraging competitive behavior and discouraging cohesive behavior) are conducive to an employee's working as fast as he can,
which is perceived as "competing" by others in the group.
This perception results in intragroup conflict which is not
consonant with cohesive behavior. The data support such a
causal chain.

Summary

The following findings of the first study were replicated.
Cohesive and competitive behavior emerge as separate factors

on a factor analysis. Work pressure is related positively to competitive behavior and negatively to cohesive behavior. Under high pressure the reward structure provides strong incentives for competitive behavior but not for cohesive behavior, whereas under low pressure the incentives are more for cohesive behavior. There are stronger group sanctions against competitive behavior under high pressure than under low pressure. As a consequence, when competitive behavior occurs under high pressure, it is negatively associated with cohesive behavior. This is not true under low pressure. More specifically, when competitive behavior occurs under conditions of high pressure together with unresponsive management, there is the lowest cohesive behavior.

In addition the following extension was presented. Intragroup conflict behaviors emerge as a fairly independent dimension on our factor analysis, and these behaviors are positively related to work pressure. As with cohesive behavior, intragroup conflict is highly associated with competitive behavior under high pressure but not under low pressure. This supported our assumption that competitive behavior produced intragroup conflict under high pressure and that intragroup conflict is not consonant with cohesive behavior.

CHAPTER 7

Rewards for Cohesive Behavior under High Pressure Conditions

WE HAVE NOT YET considered in detail the effects of work pressure on cohesive behavior when pressure is accompanied by rewards for cohesive behavior. In the first study we examined the relationship between rewards for cooperative behavior and pressure and found that these rewards were significantly more apt to occur under low pressure than under high pressure. However, there is only a small relationship between the magnitude of these rewards and actual cohesive behavior. We obtained approximately the same results in the replication.

In the first study we also found a strong negative relationship between work pressure and the time available to engage in cohesive behavior. Moreover, we found that the time available for cohesive behavior was significantly (though not strongly) related to the actual occurrence of cohesive behavior.[1]

These two findings together suggest that actual cohesive behavior is related to the degree of tenability of cohesive behavior. Most important, they may give us some new insight into the dynamics of cohesive behavior. For instance, we found that by and large under high work pressure the cohesive response is not apt to occur in the face of the reward structure and the tenability of the competitive response. We mentioned that this finding is similar to earlier studies (Mintz 1951, Hamblin 1958) in that when faced with individual threat, members of a group tend to respond individually if they do not perceive collective action as a way of reducing the threat. In our study populations collective action rarely occurred. Also, in dealing with employees management has always stressed the individual employee's needs. All first-level managers are exhorted to deal with employees as individuals. As a result a collective response to work pressure applied to the individual employee was probably not a habitual one.

Since we believe that our initial reasoning (i.e., threat produces needs that can be reduced by cohesiveness) has merit from both a theoretical and an empirical point of view, we must now ask the question "What happens when the cohesive response is tenable in the face of high work pressure?"

We have examined the relationship between rewards for cooperative behavior and the occurrence of such behavior and have found only a slight positive relationship between the two. Despite this, we can safely postulate that cohesive behavior should be more tenable when it is encouraged by superiors. The fact that it does not resoundingly occur in our populations might indicate that other factors are needed as catalysts. According to our initial theory, one catalyst could be the existence of a threat. Thus when work pressures and rewards for cohesive behavior from management occur together, the cohesive response could be tenable.

Another high pressure condition under which cohesive behavior could be tenable is the application of pressure on a group basis. An illustration of this kind of pressure is an athletic team. Pressure exists for individual members, but a large share of pressure is applied to the group as a whole. Most important, as each member reaches his own goals, e.g., hitting .400, even though he may be competing against others on the team, his outstanding performance enables them to reach goals of their own, e.g., winning the game.

Considering this reasoning, we make two hypotheses:

1.   Under conditions of high work pressure and high re-

[1] Unfortunately, we do not have the data available for a replication of this latter finding.

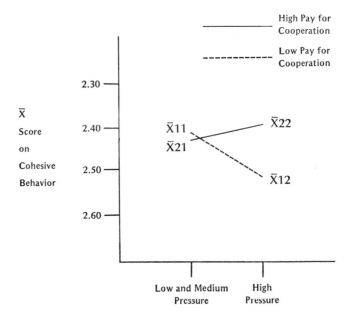

Figure 21
Relationship between Work Pressure and
Cohesive Behavior in the First Study
Controlling for Pay for Cooperation (t $\bar{X}$12, $\bar{X}$22 P<.05)

wards for cooperative behavior, there will be high cohesive behavior.

2. Under conditions of high pressure when the pressures are applied on a group basis, there will be high cohesive behavior.

We can test the first hypothesis in both studies. The second is testable only in the second study.

Test of Hypothesis 1

To test this hypothesis we broke the populations into high and low groups according to the mean score on our item measuring pay for cooperation. Using this variable as a control, we then looked at the relationship between pressure and cohesion.[2] The results are shown in Figures 21 and 22.

[2] We combined the medium and low pressure groups since they resembled each other much more than either resembled the high pressure group.

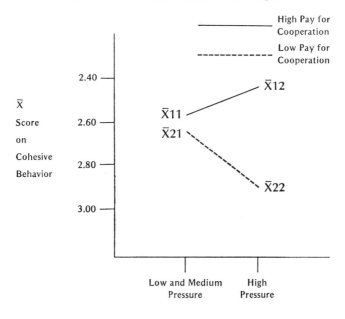

Figure 22
Relationship between Work Pressure and
Cohesive Behavior in the Second Study
Controlling for Pay for Cooperation (t $\bar{X}12$, $\bar{X}22$ P<.05)

The first hypothesis is supported in both studies, though the difference between the high pressure–high pay for cooperation group is not significantly different from other groups in the second study. However, the second study replicates almost exactly the findings of the first study.

Test of Hypothesis 2

To test this hypothesis we broke the populations into high and low groups according to the mean score on our item measuring the application of pressure on a group basis. Using this as a control, we tested for the relationship between pressure and cohesive behavior. For results see Figure 23.

While we do not have a replication of this finding, we see that in the second study those groups which are subjected to high pressure on a group basis are significantly more cohesive than those which are not.

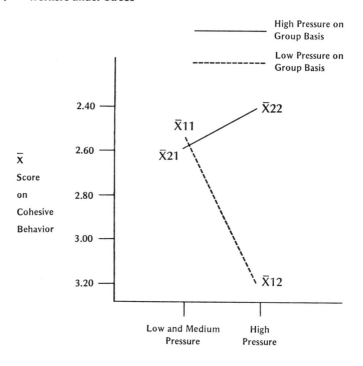

Figure 23
Relationship between Work Pressure and
Cohesive Behavior in the Second Study Controlling for
Pressure Applied on Group Basis (t $\bar{X}12$, $\bar{X}22$ P<.01)

Both hypotheses are supported. Under high pressure, rewards for cooperation and application of pressure on a group
basis are both associated with higher cohesive behavior. The
fact that under low and medium pressure these variables are
not associated with cohesive behavior suggests that they are
not powerful variables by themselves. However, in interaction with high work pressure they produce a marked effect
on cohesive behavior. Thus, theoretically, cohesive behavior
may be partly a function of work pressure, but only under
specific rewarding conditions.

We must still examine the conditioning effects of the rewards for group behavior on the relationship between work
pressure and competitive behavior. If we find that the competitive response is not stifled to any great extent under high

pressure when there are high rewards for group behavior, more of our theory may be pertinent. In other words, if cohesive behaviors can still prevail when there are powerful incentives for competitive behavior as well as strong group sanctions against competitive behavior, then our conclusion that work pressure is associated with group cohesion under appropriate rewarding conditions is further supported. We will test this reasoning by examining the effects on competitive behavior of rewards for cooperation and of pressure applied on a group basis. The results follow in Figures 24, 25, and 26.

Each of these figures illustrates that competitive behavior under high pressure is affected neither by rewards for cooperation nor by pressure applied on a group basis. Under high pressure there is little or no difference between the high and low controls. Moreover, competitive behavior still oc-

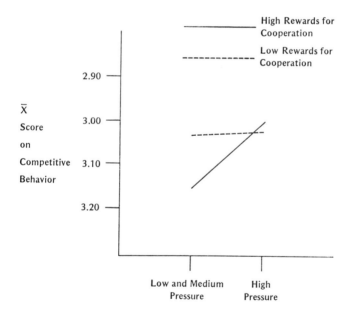

Figure 24
Relationship between Work Pressure and
Competitive Behavior in the First Study
Controlling for Rewards for Cooperation

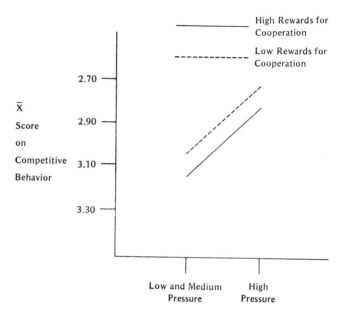

Figure 25
Relationship between Work Pressure and
Competitive Behavior in the Second Study
Controlling for Rewards for Cooperation

curs more frequently under high pressure than under the other pressure conditions, regardless of controls. Thus the above assumption is supported.

The most interesting thing that emerges from this series of analyses is that under high pressure, if there are high rewards for group behavior, competitive and cohesive behaviors occur together. There may be at least two reasons for this. First, the managers who reward on a group basis provide at the same time a setting in which competitive behavior is less threatening. Second, by emphasizing group goals as well as individual goals such managers are making the two kinds of goals more compatible. As a result, when an employee engages in competitive behavior to serve his own goals he is at the same time helping others to move toward the group goals and thus increasing the probability of cohesive behavior. Let and is therefore increasing the probability of cohesive behavior. Let us now examine each of these conditions in more detail.

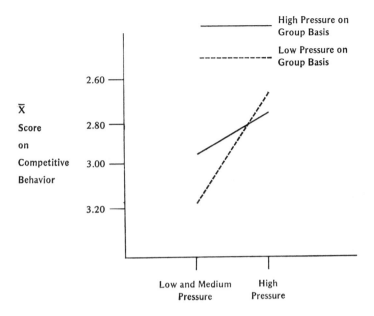

Figure 26
Relationship between Work Pressure and
Competitive Behavior in the Second Study
Controlling for Pressure Applied on a Group Basis

Manager Provides Less Threatening Environment

We found that under high pressure when managers are responsive to the needs of their employees, there is less dislike of competitive behavior and more cohesive behavior when competitive behavior does occur than when managers are unresponsive (see Figures 13 and 14). In both studies we find a significant correlation between rewards for cooperation and responsiveness of management ($r = .46$ in the first study and $r = .44$ in the second study). Thus there is some tendency for managers who pay for cooperation also to provide opportunities for employees to influence productivity expectations; these managers thereby provide a less threatening environment in which competitive behavior may occur. However, the correlation between pressure applied on a group basis and responsive management is only .10 (data available in the second study only). Thus the unthreatening environment explains only one facet of the obtained data.

Compatibility of Group and Individual Goals

Deutsch (1949) created two experimental conditions. The first involved what he called "promotive interdependence," which means that when one member of a group moved toward his own goal, this constituted a similar movement for all others in that group toward their own goals. The second condition involved "contrient interdependence," which means that when one member moved toward an individual goal, this was a deprivation for others in that group.

Thomas (1957) created four experimental conditions. Three involved varying degrees of "facilitative role interdependence," i.e., the movement of one person in the group toward a goal to some extent helped the others in the group move toward a goal. The fourth, in which people worked toward their own goals, involved no interdependence.

Both Thomas and Deutsch found that under conditions in which the movement of one person toward a goal meant that others too would move toward the goal, there was more cohesive behavior than when the individual movement meant deprivation or lack of movement for the others.

In our situation, when pressure is applied on a group basis (e.g., a high group goal is set up) as well as on an individual basis, competitive behavior could be instrumental in obtaining both individual and group goals. If high pressure is applied solely on an individual basis, when an individual reaches the goal by working fast he reduces pressure only for himself and may in fact increase the pressure for the others by demonstrating that the goals are achievable. On the other hand, by applying pressure on a group basis a manager can bring group goals and individual goals into closer harmony and thereby reduce the potential intragroup conflict. Under these conditions, when individuals compete they help others in addition to helping themselves and thus increase the probability of cohesive behaviors.

Summary

We found that under high pressure when managers reward for cooperative behavior or apply pressure on a group basis, there is high cohesive behavior as well as high competitive behavior. We suggested two possible reasons for this. First, managers who reward for group behavior are likely to provide a situation in which competitive behavior is not threatening. This is partially supported by the data. Second, managers who emphasize group goals as well as individual goals bring these two goals closer together. This occurs because competitive behavior is in the service of group goals as well as individual goals and therefore is less productive of intragroup conflict. There is no data to test this latter reasoning adequately, though two past studies provide supporting evidence.

CHAPTER 8

Discussion and Summary

IT IS CLEAR that for the most part high work pressure as we have defined it is associated with low cohesive behavior. While the degree of association is not large, it is statistically significant in both studies. We have suggested that an important reason for this is that the reward structure defined by management encourages competitive behavior in the high pressure condition and that this behavior is internally threatening to the group because quantity of production is extremely important and because by definition many people in high pressure groups have difficulty turning out the required amount. Anyone who "tries to work faster" than others potentially jeopardizes the position of those who cannot turn out the required amount. This reasoning can be summarized in the following way:

1. High pressure is associated with competitive behavior because the reward structure imposed by management encourages people to work as fast as they can individually.
2. Under high pressure, competitive behavior is threatening and thus is associated with intragroup conflict.
3. Intragroup conflict is negatively associated with cohesive behavior.
4. Therefore high pressure is negatively associated with cohesive behavior.

This reasoning is substantiated in both studies. We found that when competition occurs in groups under high pressure, there is the least cohesive behavior, though competition has no such association in the other pressure groups.

Moreover, in the second study and by implication in the first study, we found that competition has a similar relationship with intragroup conflict. Schematically, using product-moment correlations in the high and low pressure groups of the second study,[1] the results look like this:

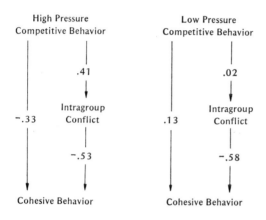

Figure 27
Relationships among Group Behaviors under
High and Low Work Pressure

Thus we see that under high pressure, competition is related to both intragroup conflict and cohesive behavior, whereas under low pressure it is not. However, when we take the total population and derive first-order partial correlations, we find that there may be no direct relationship between competitive behavior and cohesive behavior but rather that competitive behavior has to produce intragroup conflict, which in turn is always associated with low cohesive behavior. Witness the scheme shown in Figure 28 using first-order partials controlling for one class of behavior while determining the relationship between the other two.

The r between competitive behavior and cohesive behavior controlling for group conflict is reduced from −.24 to −.01. The r between competitive behavior and intragroup conflict is reduced from .41 to .34. The r between conflict

[1] We do not have a measure of intragroup conflict in the first study.

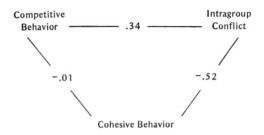

Figure 28
Partial Correlations among Group Behaviors

and cohesive behavior is reduced from −.56 to −.52. This scheme tends to support the reasoning that competitive behavior must first produce intragroup conflict, which in turn is negatively associated with cohesive behavior.

Direction of Causality

We have postulated a causal chain running from high pressure to competitive behavior to intragroup conflict, which in turn is always negatively associated with cohesive behavior. In this study we used data collected at one point in time and relied heavily on correlational analysis, so we cannot be sure of the direction of causality. We make the well-substantiated assumption that pressure is our independent variable, but other things are less clear.

As we have stated, it is entirely plausible that when pressure is applied to groups low in cohesive behavior, the members of these groups will respond with competitive behavior, whereas under low pressure there is no reason to be competitive regardless of the cohesive nature of the group. However, except for invoking a circular reasoning (i.e., competition produces more intragroup conflict and less cohesive behavior), this does not explain why there is more intragroup conflict and less cohesive behavior in the high pressure group nor why the longer the group is under pressure, the less cohesive behavior it displays. It only explains why there is a negative relationship between competitive and cohesive behavior under high pressure—particularly since there is no reason to suspect that pressure was applied first to low cohesive groups.

The Concept of Group Cohesiveness

Initially we assumed that group cohesiveness was a variable that could be predicted on the basis of its instrumentality for satisfying needs created by work pressure. We have demonstrated that in our population and with our measurements this may not be the case. In fact our evidence suggests that group cohesiveness occurs because nothing impedes it or because it is encouraged by management rather than because it has inherent instrumental characteristics.

For instance, we found cohesive behavior to occur in the absence of threatening competitive behavior or when competitive behavior served group goals as well as individual goals. In no sense can one interpret our data by considering cohesive behavior as a powerful instrumental act that somehow made things better in the face of work pressure. When the reward structure imposed by management served to destroy it, it was in fact destroyed. Only when the management-imposed reward structure was consonant with the existence of cohesive behavior did cohesive behavior in fact exist. In no case did cohesive behavior under high pressure rise substantially above the level of that found under low pressure. Since in the low pressure condition cohesive behavior had the least impedimenta, we must consider that in our population cohesive behavior occurred in the absence of inhibition rather than in the presence of some environmental force that cohesive behavior might affect.

In each of the previously reported studies showing group integration resulting from threat, the integrative responses were rewarding. For instance, Brophy's seamen (1946) depended on each other for survival as did Grinker and Spiegel's bomber crews (1945). If these groups had not closely cooperated their lives would have been in danger. In each of these situations cohesive behavior was a positive instrumental response that was required in order for individuals to survive. In our industrial situation, on the other hand, individual goals were stressed under work pressure, and only when group goals were also stressed could cohesive behavior be maintained.

Perhaps a more basic question involves the importance of the variable cohesiveness itself. Festinger et al. (1950), Back (1951), Cartwright and Zander (1968), Lott and Lott (1965), Byrne (1969), and others have considered cohesiveness a variable of central significance. While this may be so with some groups and in some instances, it may not be the case in the industrial environment when other variables are considered. As mentioned earlier, Seashore (1954) found low correlations between cohesiveness and all the other variables he was dealing with even though many relationships were highly significant. Generally we found the same thing to be true.

For instance, in regard to the possible effects of cohesiveness—a subject we do not treat in this study—we find only marginal relationships. The correlation between cohesive behavior and mental illness symptoms is only $-.23$, and the correlation between cohesiveness and absenteeism is even less. When we control for pressure, these correlations reduce to less than .10.

In addition recall that we found a high positive correlation between the occurrence of competitive behavior and the dislike of competitive behavior. Apart from considerations of the degree of cohesiveness as a conditioner of this relationship, it is hard to imagine that given a power within the group to suppress competitive behavior effectively, such behavior would not be suppressed when it becomes extremely threatening. The fact that it is not suppressed suggests that the power of the group compared to the power of other factors, such as the reward structure designed by management, is rather limited. Perhaps only when groups are extremely cohesive can they effectively stifle threatening behavior that is individually oriented and strongly motivated.

Our data only hint at the resolutions of these questions, but the issues are all subject to empirical investigation.

Reevaluation of Some Previous Research

We have mentioned that Seashore (1954) and Buck (1963) found a negative relationship between feelings of pressure and cohesiveness in an industrial context. They suggested that people in cohesive groups feel less pressure because they derive social support or some other intangible benefit that is not available in groups lacking cohesion. In addition Seashore, as well as Likert (1961),[2] found that feelings of nervousness and tenseness were negatively associated with cohesion. Our findings show exactly the same relationship, but according to our interpretation it occurs for different reasons.

We find that the extent of feelings of pressure is a direct consequence of the amount of pressure applied by management. According to the causal chain we have suggested, the degree of cohesiveness is indirectly the consequence of the amount of pressure applied.[3] If this is so, then feelings of pressure and group cohesiveness are both affected by objective pressure, and consequently the relationship between them may be spurious. Thus, instead of cohesiveness somehow reducing feelings of pressure, we suggest that the natural antecedent of feelings of pressure—namely, actual pressure applied—affects both feelings of pressure and cohesiveness and that there may be no direct relationship between the two consequent variables. Exactly the same logic holds for feelings of nervousness and tenseness. The resolution of this question awaits further research.

[2] Likert does not study cohesion as such. His variable is group loyalty, and the manager is included as part of the group.

[3] Seashore attempted to control for objective pressure by forming his groups according to actual productivity level. His reasoning was that groups low in productivity would be under more pressure. However, we find that there is a positive relationship between amounts of pressure applied and productivity. Our high pressure groups in fact had slightly higher productivity than the other groups.

Some Limitations of This Study

Part of this study involved a systematic replication. Because of this we have some confidence that the results are reliable and to some extent can be generalized. They are reliable because, apart from the significance of the statistical tests, for the most part we have repeated the results of the first study in the second study, using the same procedure and dealing with the same classes of variables.

More important, there is a good indication that our results can be generalized to some extent since the replication was conducted in a population that was subjected to work pressure in a different way, had different cultural characteristics, and was composed of a different mix of skills. Also the measure of pressure was somewhat different, and we extended the study to include a direct measure of an effect we indirectly showed to exist in the first study. Nevertheless, there are some limits to possible generalization about our results.

For instance, we don't know if the same kinds of relationships would obtain in a unionized organization, where a group response is more institutionalized. Nor do we know if they would obtain where management does not have the history of benevolence characteristic of the company we studied. Perhaps different occupational groups, such as engineers, technicians, and schoolteachers, would react differently to work pressures. Further, because our data appear to contradict a considerable body of evidence suggesting that shared threat tends to coalesce rather than fractionate groups, we must be cautious when we extrapolate these findings to nonindustrialized, homogeneous groups whose members share characteristics such as race or ethnic background. Generalizations can be made only in light of the individual responses available to each group member faced with threat. If the adaptive response for threat reduction is coalescence, then that will likely occur. It is not difficult to imagine examples of this response. On the other hand, if the adaptive response is perceived to be individual behavior that threatens the group integrity, then one might expect a reduction in group cohesion.

In addition to the problem of generalization, two other problems are inherent in the survey method. First, the method of collecting data at one point in time is not amenable to unraveling cause and effect. Often, as in our case, one can be reasonably sure of an independent variable and by fiat declare what is to be the dependent variable. However, one can never be sure that some other unspecified and unknown intervening or conditioning variable related to both the dependent and the independent variable is not causing the main effect. This problem may exist in the lab but to a much lesser extent. Moreover, as we have mentioned before, after we get past the independent variable the causal chain is often unclear.

A second problem is "halo effect." Basically our independent, conditioning, and criterion variables are derived from the same measuring instrument. Consequently we can never be sure that they are related in the way we suggest, or that they are related at all, because of a response bias of unknown strength that probably exists. We have in some measure overcome this problem by using groups as our unit of analysis and thus reducing individual response bias. Nevertheless, because the differences we find are often small, a few individuals in a group could affect the group mean enough to affect the results. These problems can largely be overcome by extending this study to include other occupational groups, other organizations, and different study designs.

Implications for Future Research

The Rational Man Concept

We have shown generally how group cohesiveness can be inhibited and perhaps destroyed if a reward structure produces individually oriented behavior that is threatening to others in the group. Yet we have also shown that good social relationships and cooperative behavior may be goals in themselves. Thus one of the things this study implies is a conflict in goals since the attainment of one set of goals (economic and organizational well-being as defined and supported by management) implies the lack of or only partial attainment of another (maintaining friendly and cooperative group relations).

The attainment of organizational goals follows well-defined paths. These paths are laid out by the organization's power figures, who provide predictable, easily stated, and easily understood incentives. They equate increases in pay and greater opportunities to attain desirable jobs with increases in individual productivity: the instrumental act is simply to increase the employee's productivity. This involves his working faster, which is perceived by others in the group as competitive behavior. Because many people can increase their productivity and because this is seen as a way of attaining the organizational set of goals, the instrumental act (i.e., competitive behavior) becomes a realistic response.

The opposing set of goals involves maintaining pleasant, cooperative relationships within the group. These goals are defined by peers, and in our high pressure group they would require the inhibition of a response that would lead to the attainment of the first set of goals. The fact that this inhibition does not occur is not surprising for at least two reasons: the power of the rewarding agent is not as great and the rewards themselves are not as important. In other words, competitive behavior seems a more rational response than the inhibition of it, and its occurrence under high pressure suggests rational behavior.

Further support for this "rational man" argument is offered by our finding that when cohesive behavior does occur under high pressure, it is usually accompanied by rewards from management for behaving cohesively. This reasoning should be tested in other circumstances and in other ways so that a more comprehensive theory can be developed to help explain and predict behavior in organization. For example, Vroom (1964) and Porter and Lawler (1968) have advanced an "Expectancy Theory" that, simply stated, predicts behavior on the basis of expected positive or negative outcomes multiplied by probabilities of the outcomes occurring, given certain behavior. While values of rewards and probabilities of reward occurrence are exceedingly difficult to determine, behaviors may be predicted according to the product of the values of the two classes of variables. This is much the same as the instrumental position we advanced initially and supported when the relative importance of the variables was deduced. Strong support for a theory of this nature was presented when we sorted out the rewarding conditions and showed that cohesive behavior resulted when managers rewarded such behavior, thus adding incentive above that provided by social and protective need satisfaction. Thus in a sense people "expected" to be rewarded for cohesive behavior. Cohesiveness took on added value and probabilities and therefore was more likely to occur. In this way our instrumental theory and expectancy theory are virtually indistinguishable since both involve the value of rewards and the likelihood that certain behaviors will lead to such rewards. The problem then becomes the specification of values of competing outcomes and the probabilities that competing responses will achieve these outcomes.

The Delicate Fabric of Cohesiveness

Our results indicate that group cohesive behavior is a somewhat tenuous condition. Much previous work has emphasized the causes of cohesive behavior, whereas this study of necessity has emphasized the causes of its lack. If cohesive behavior is a desirable condition, then perhaps a fruitful avenue of research might involve the specification of maintenance forces for cohesiveness in the face of centrifugal forces such as we found in this study. A start in this direction is provided by our and others' findings that when goals are such that a person's movement toward his own goals also encourages others' movement toward their goals, then group cohesive behavior can be maintained even in the face of strong individual incentives.

Summary

This study investigated the effects of work pressure on group cohesion in industrial work groups. Only "induced" work pressure was considered. Group cohesion was considered to be the consequence of specific behaviors engaged in by group members. These behaviors were measured by reports of the group members themselves about how others in the group acted.

Our original theoretical position was that work pressure would lead to threat and anxieties associated with threat and to loss of environmental control by the worker. This reasoning was confirmed. Most important, however, we believed that these factors would arouse needs which could be satisfied by cohesive behavior. Thus our basic hypothesis stated that work pressure would produce group cohesive behavior. Generally we found just the opposite. There were several major findings.

Behaviors which can be considered theoretically to affect group cohesion fall into two independent dimensions: social-supportive behavior and competitive behavior. A third class of behavior that correlates moderately well with both the social-supportive behavior and the competitive behavior but which falls on a fairly independent factor of its own is intragroup conflict behavior. Work pressure in general is negatively related to social-supportive behavior, which we have called cohesive behavior, and positively related to competitive and intragroup conflict behavior.

Cohesive behavior is generally untenable under high pressure conditions because the reward structure imposed by management directs employees to work as fast as they can individually. Competitive behavior, on the other hand, is thereby encouraged. In addition we found that cohesive behavior is quite tenable under low pressure conditions due to the reward structure and to the fact that there is more time to engage in cohesive behavior.

When competitive behavior occurs under high pressure, it is positively associated with intragroup conflict and negatively associated with cohesive behavior, but there is little or no association between competitive behavior and these other two behaviors under conditions of low pressure. We suggested that the reason for this is that competitive behavior is threatening to group members only under high pressure conditions where quantity of work is important and where people have trouble turning out the appropriate quantity. Thus when competitive behavior does occur under high pressure, it is associated with intragroup conflict, which is not consonant with cohesive behavior. This reasoning is supported by the data.

The only data supporting our original theory resulted when managers rewarded group behavior under high pressure. Then there was a marked increment in cohesive behavior even though there was no decrement in competitive behavior. This result was interpreted to be a function of two conditions: Managers who reward for cooperative behavior tend to create an environment in which competitive behavior can occur without being threatening, and managers who apply pressure on a group basis bring group goals more in line with individual goals, thereby making an approach to individual goals (through competitive behavior) serve common interests.

APPENDIX A

Some Statistical Procedures

Procedure for Factor Analysis

The mean scores for 172 departments in the first study and 111 departments in the second study on 55 bipolar items were computed. These scores were then intercorrelated, using the Pearson product moment method. The square matrix of correlation coefficients served as the basis for factor analysis. Communalities were then computed. The principal components of the resulting matrix were extracted and an oblique rotation was performed on the first seven factors, using Carroll's biquartinin criterion with gamma equal to .5.

Scale of Cohesiveness in the Second Study

The cohesive behavior scale in the second study was stretched to a ten-point scale. (All the cohesive behavior items were combined into a scale by computer and the only index-forming program available was based on a ten-point scale.) All the first study computations were done with a desk calculator except the factor analysis, to which the "stretching out" does not apply. The stretching computation follows: $x - 1 \cdot \dfrac{10}{\text{old range} - 1}$.

APPENDIX B

Statistical Details

TABLE 14
ANALYSES OF VARIANCE FOR FIGURES IN CHAPTER 4

	S.S.	df	Mean Square Variance	F
Figure 2				
Between-class	.36	2	.18	3.33†
Within-class	8.02	147	.054	
Figure 3				
Between-class	.37	2	.185	2.51*
Within-class	10.83	147	.074	
Figure 6				
High job control				
Between-class	.27	2	.135	2.39*
Within-class	4.23	75	.056	
Low job control				
Between-class	.01	2	.005	.104
Within-class	3.33	69	.048	
Figure 7				
High job control				
Between-class	.22	2	.11	1.10
Within-class	7.53	75	.10	
Low job control				
Between-class	.17	2	.085	1.88
Within-class	3.11	69	.045	
Figure 8				
Good grievance channels				
Between-class	.17	2	.085	1.70
Within-class	3.12	62	.050	

	S.S.	df	Mean Square Variance	F
Poor grievance channels				
Between-class	.22	2	.11	1.97
Within-class	4.59	82	.056	
Figure 9				
Good grievance channels				
Between-class	.09	2	.045	.608
Within-class	4.59	62	.074	
Poor grievance channels				
Between-class	.15	2	.075	1.04
Within-class	5.92	82	.072	
Figure 10				
Stable standards				
Between-class	.30	2	.15	3.43†
Within-class	3.46	79	.044	
Unstable standards				
Between-class	.34	2	.17	2.75*
Within-class	4.02	65	.062	
Figure 11				
Stable standards				
Between-class	.05	2	.025	.268
Within-class	6.05	65	.093	
Unstable standards				
Between-class	.19	2	.095	1.83
Within-class	4.11	79	.052	

* $P < .10$
† $P < .05$

TABLE 15

TESTS FOR DIFFERENCES IN MEANS
AS REPORTED IN CHAPTER 4

	$\bar{X}$	S.D. $\bar{X}_1-\bar{X}_2$	P
Figure 4			
High pressure			
Long time under	2.52	.069	.10
Short time under	2.40		

TABLE 15 *continued*

	$\bar{X}$	S.D. $\bar{X}1-\bar{X}2$	P
Figure 6			
High job control	2.36	.036	<.01
Low job control	2.48		
Figure 7			
High job control	3.14	.0437	<.001
Low job control	2.99		
Figure 8			
Good grievance channels	2.37	.036	<.02
Poor grievance channels	2.46		
Figure 9			
Good grievance channels	3.13	.0435	<.02
Poor grievance channels	2.97		
Figure 10			
Stable standards	2.38	.036	<.05
Unstable standards	2.46		
Figure 11			
Stable standards	3.13	.0435	<.01
Unstable standards	2.99		

TABLE 16

ANALYSIS OF VARIANCE FOR FIGURE 7 IN CHAPTER 4

High Competition	S.S.	df	Mean Square Variance	F
Between-class	.41	2	.205	3.53*
Within-class	3.84	66	.058	

* < .05

TABLE 17

TEST FOR DIFFERENCE IN COHESIVE BEHAVIOR
BETWEEN HIGH AND LOW COMPETITIVE GROUPS
UNDER HIGH PRESSURE (FIGURE 12, CHAPTER 5)

High Pressure	$\bar{X}$	S.D. $\bar{X}1-\bar{X}2$	P
High competition	2.53	.0678	<.05
Low competition	2.39		

TABLE 18

MEAN SCORE STANDARD DEVIATION AND P VALUE
OF DATA REPORTED IN FIGURES 13, 14, AND 15
IN CHAPTER 5

	$\bar{X}$	S.D. of diff.	P
Figure 13			
Unresponsive mgt.-high pressure ($\bar{X}1$)	3.00	$\bar{X}1 - \bar{X}2$ .16	N.S.
Responsive mgt.-high pressure ($\bar{X}2$)	3.23		
Unresponsive mgt.-other pressure ($\bar{X}3$)	3.24	$\bar{X}1 - \bar{X}3$ .12	<.05
Responsive mgt.-other pressure ($\bar{X}4$)	3.41	$\bar{X}1 - \bar{X}4$ .11	<.01
Figure 14			
Unresponsive mgt.-high pressure ($\bar{X}1$)	2.96	$\bar{X}1 - \bar{X}2$ .078	<.05
Responsive mgt.-high pressure ($\bar{X}2$)	3.12		
Unresponsive mgt.-other pressure ($\bar{X}3$)	3.05	$\bar{X}1 - \bar{X}3$ .069	N.S.
Responsive mgt.-other pressure ($\bar{X}4$)	3.13	$\bar{X}1 - \bar{X}4$ .065	<.02

TABLE 18 *continued*

	$\bar{X}$	S.D. of diff.	P
Figure 15			
High pressure-			
high competition			
Unresponsive mgt. ($\bar{X}1$)	2.64	$\bar{X}1 - \bar{X}2$ .0824	<.001
Responsive mgt. ($\bar{X}2$)	2.32		
High pressure-			
low competition			
Unresponsive mgt. ($\bar{X}3$)	2.42	$\bar{X}1 - \bar{X}3$ .0648	<.01
Responsive mgt. ($\bar{X}4$)	2.34	$\bar{X}1 - \bar{X}4$ .104	<.001

TABLE 19

MEAN SCORE STANDARD DEVIATION AND P VALUE
OF DATA REPORTED IN FIGURES 18 AND 20
IN CHAPTER 6

	$\bar{X}$	S.D. of diff.	P
Figure 18			
High competition			
Low pressure ($\bar{X}1$)	2.51		
Medium pressure ($\bar{X}2$)	2.95		
High pressure ($\bar{X}3$)	2.92		
Low competition			
Low pressure ($\bar{X}4$)	2.45		
Medium pressure ($\bar{X}5$)	2.60	$\bar{X}2 - \bar{X}5$ .29	N.S.
High pressure ($\bar{X}6$)	2.32	$\bar{X}3 - \bar{X}6$ .33	<.10
Figure 20			
High competition			
Low pressure ($\bar{X}1$)	7.58		
Medium pressure ($\bar{X}2$)	6.74		
High pressure ($\bar{X}3$)	6.72		
Low competition			
Low pressure ($\bar{X}4$)	7.53		
Medium pressure ($\bar{X}5$)	7.47	$\bar{X}2 - \bar{X}5$ .306	<.05
High pressure ($\bar{X}6$)	7.70	$\bar{X}3 - \bar{X}6$ .37	<.02

TABLE 20

MEAN SCORE STANDARD DEVIATION AND P VALUE
OF DATA REPORTED IN FIGURES 21, 22, AND 23
IN CHAPTER 7

	$\bar{X}$	S.D. of diff.	P
Figure 21			
High pay for cooperation			
High pressure ($\bar{X}1$)	2.37		
Other pressure ($\bar{X}2$)	2.39		
Low pay for cooperation			
High pressure ($\bar{X}3$)	2.51	$\bar{X}3 - \bar{X}1$ .068	$<.05$
Other pressure ($\bar{X}4$)	2.40		
Figure 22			
High pay for cooperation			
High pressure ($\bar{X}1$)	2.48		
Other pressure ($\bar{X}2$)	2.56		
Low pay for cooperation			
High pressure ($\bar{X}3$)	2.90	$\bar{X}3 - \bar{X}1$ .30	N.S.
Other pressure ($\bar{X}4$)	2.64		
Figure 23			
High pressure			
on group basis			
High pressure ($\bar{X}1$)	2.44		
Other pressure ($\bar{X}2$)	2.59		
Low pressure			
on group basis			
High pressure ($\bar{X}3$)	3.25	$\bar{X}3 - \bar{X}1$ .248	$<.01$
Other pressure ($\bar{X}4$)	2.57		

APPENDIX C

Relationships between Work Pressure
and Individual Items in the Cohesiveness Index:
First Study

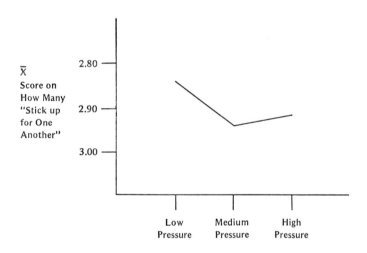

Figure 29
Relationship between Work Pressure and How Many
"Stick up for One Another" (F=3.65, P<.05)

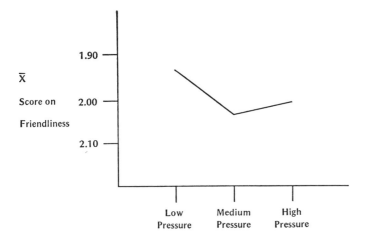

Figure 30
Relationship between Work Pressure and
Friendliness (F=7.87, P<.01)

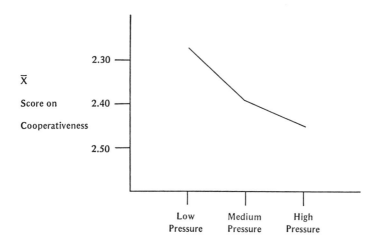

Figure 31
Relationship between Work Pressure and
Cooperativeness (F=3.33, P<.05)

REFERENCES

Argyris, C. *Integrating the Individual and the Organization.* New York: John Wiley & Sons, 1964.

——. *Personality and Organization.* New York: Harper and Bros., 1957.

Atkinson, J. W., and Reitman, W. R. "Performance as a Function of Motive Strength and Expectancy of Goal Attainment." *Journal of Abnormal and Social Psychology* 53 (1956) : 361–66.

Back, K. "Influence Through Social Communication." *Journal of Abnormal and Social Psychology* 46 (1951) : 9–23.

Bass, B. *Leadership, Psychology, and Organizational Behavior.* New York: Harper and Bros., 1960.

Blalock, H. M. *Social Statistics.* New York: McGraw-Hill, 1960.

Brophy, I. M. "The Luxury of Anti-Negro Prejudices." *Public Opinion Quarterly* 10 (1946) : 456–66.

Buck, V. E. "Job Pressures on Managers, Sources, Subjects and Correlates." Ph.D. dissertation, Cornell University, 1963.

Burnstein, E., and McRae, Adie. "Some Effects of Shared Threat and Prejudice in Racially Mixed Groups." *Journal of Abnormal and Social Psychology* 64 (1962) :257–63.

Byrne, D. "Attitudes and Attraction." In *Advances in Experimental Social Psychology,* edited by L. Berkowitz, pp. 36–90. New York: Academic Press, 1969.

Carey, A. "The Hawthorne Studies: A Radical Criticism." *American Sociological Review* 32 (1967) : 403–16.

Cartwright, D., and Zander, A., eds. *Group Dynamics: Research and Theory.* 3d ed. Evanston, Ill.: Row, Petterson, 1968.

Deutsch, M. "The Effects of Cooperation and Competition upon Group Process." In *Group Dynamics: Research and Theory,* edited by D. Cartwright and A. Zander, pp. 414–48. 2d ed. Evanston, Ill.: Row, Petterson, 1960.

113

Dollard, J., Doob, L. W., Miller, N. E., Mower, O. H., and Sears, R. R. *Frustration and Aggression*. New Haven, Conn.: Yale University Press, 1939.

Doob, L. W. "The Behavior of Attitudes." *Psychological Review* 54 (1947) : 135–56.

Downing, J. "Cohesiveness, Perception and Values." *Human Relations* 11 (1958) : 157–66.

Eisman, Bernice. "Some Operational Measures of Cohesiveness and Their Correlations." *Human Relations* 12 (1959) : 183–89.

Festinger, L., Back, K., Schachter, S., Kelley, H., and Thibaut, J. *Theory and Experiment in Social Communication*. Ann Arbor, Mich.: Institute for Social Research, 1950.

Festinger, L., Schachter, S., and Back, K. *Social Pressures in Informal Groups*. New York: Harper and Bros., 1950.

Fouriezos, N., Hutt, M., and Guetzkow, H. "Measurement of Self Oriented Needs in Discussion Groups." *Journal of Abnormal and Social Psychology* 45 (1950) : 682–89.

French, J. R. P., Jr. "The Disruption and Cohesion of Groups." *Journal of Abnormal and Social Psychology* 36 (1941) : 361–77.

Golden, C. S., and Ruttenberg, H. J. *The Dynamics of Industrial Democracy*. New York: Harper and Bros., 1942.

Grinker, R., and Spiegel, J. *Men under Stress*. Philadelphia: Blakiston, 1945.

Gross, N., and Martin, W. "On Cohesiveness." *American Journal of Sociology* 57 (1952) : 533–46.

Hagood, Margurete, and Price, D. *Statistics for Sociologists*. Rev. ed. New York: Henry Holt, 1952.

Hall, C. S., and Lindzey, G. *Theories of Personality*. New York: John Wiley and Sons, 1957.

Hamblin, R. "Group Integration during a Crisis." *Human Relations* 11 (1958) : 67–76.

Hartley, E. L., and Hartley, Ruth. *The Fundamentals of Social Psychology*. New York: Alfred A. Knopf, 1955.

Herzberg, F., Mausner, B., Peterson, R., and Capwell, Dora. *Job Attitudes: Review of Research and Opinion*. Pittsburgh, Pa., Psychological Service of Pittsburgh, 1957.

Hickson, D. J. "Motives of Work People Who Restrict Their Output." *Occupational Psychology* 35 (1961) : 111–21.

Homans, G. C. *Social Behavior: Its Elementary Forms*. New York: Harcourt, Brace and World, 1961.

Jackson, J. M. "Reference Group Processes in a Formal Organization." *Sociometry* 22 (1959) : 304–27.

Janis, I. L. *Psychological Stress.* New York: John Wiley, 1958.

Jellison, J. M., and Zeisset, P. T. "Attraction as a Function of the Commonality and Desirability of a Trait Shared with Another." *Journal of Personality and Social Psychology* 11 (1969) : 115–20.

Klein, S. M., and Ritti, R. R. "Work Pressure, Supervisory Behavior and Employee Attitudes: A Factor Analysis." *Personnel Psychology* 23 (1970) : 153–67.

Lanzetta, J. "Group Behavior under Stress." *Human Relations* 8 (1955) : 29–52.

Leighton, A. *The Governing of Men.* Princeton, N.J.: Princeton University Press, 1945.

Likert, R. *New Patterns of Management.* New York: McGraw-Hill, 1961.

———. *The Human Organization.* New York: McGraw-Hill, 1967.

Linton, R. *Study of Man: An Introduction.* New York: Appleton-Century-Crofts, 1936.

Lott, A. J., et al. "The Affect of Delayed Reward on the Development of Positive Attitudes toward Persons." *Journal of Experimental Social Psychology* 5 (1969) : 101–13.

Lott, A. J., and Lott, B. E. "Group Cohesiveness and Individual Learning," *Journal of Educational Psychology* 57 (1966) : 61–73.

———. "Group Cohesiveness as Interpersonal Attraction: A Review of Relationships with Antecedent and Consequent Variables." *Psychological Bulletin* 64 (1965) : 259–309.

———. "Group Cohesiveness, Communication Level and Conformity." *Journal of Abnormal and Social Psychology* 62 (1961) : 408–12.

———. "A Learning Theory Approach to Interpersonal Attitudes." In A. G. Greenwald, T. C. Brock, and T. M. Ostrom, eds. *Psychological Foundations of Attitudes.* New York: Academic Press, 1968.

Lott, A. J.; Lott, Bernice E.; and Matthews, Gail N. "Interpersonal Attraction among Children as a Function of Vicarious Reward." *Journal of Educational Psychology* 60 (1969) : 274–83.

Lott, Bernice. "Group Cohesiveness: Learning Phenomenon." *Journal of Social Psychology* 55 (1961) : 275–86.

Lott, Bernice, and Lott, A. J. "The Formation of Positive Attitudes toward Group Members." *Journal of Abnormal and Social Psychology* 61 (1960) : 297–300.

McGregor, D. *The Human Side of the Enterprise.* New York: McGraw-Hill, 1960.

Miller, N. E., and Dollard, J. *Social Learning and Imitation.* New Haven, Conn.: Yale University Press, 1941.

Mintz, A. "Non-Adaptive Group Behavior." *Journal of Abnormal and Social Psychology* 46 (1951) : 150–59.

Myers, A. "Team Competition, Success, and the Adjustment of Group Members." *Journal of Abnormal and Social Psychology* 65 (1962) : 325–32.

Newcomb, T. M. *The Acquaintance Process.* New York: Holt, Rinehart, and Winston, 1961.

———. "Varieties of Interpersonal Attraction." In *Group Dynamics: Research and Theory,* edited by D. Cartwright and A. Zander, pp. 104–19. 2d ed. Evanston, Ill.: Row, Petterson, 1960.

Pepitone, A., and Klciner, R. "The Effects of Threat and Frustration on Group Cohesiveness." *Journal of Abnormal and Social Psychology* 54 (1957) : 192–99.

Pepitone, A., and Reichling, G. "Group Cohesiveness and the Expression of Hostility." *Human Relations* 8 (1955) : 327–37.

Perlman, M. *Labor Union Theories in America.* Evanston, Ill.: Row, Petterson, 1958.

Porter, L., and Lawler, E. E., III. *Managerial Attitudes and Performance.* Homewood, Ill.: R. D. Irwin, 1968.

Rabbie, J. M. "Differential Preference for Companionship under Threat." *Journal of Abnormal and Social Psychology* 67 (1963) : 643–48.

Raven, B., and Rietsema, J. "The Effects of Varied Clarity of Group Goal in Group Path upon the Individual and His Relation to His Group." *Human Relations* 10 (1957) : 29–44.

Roethlisberger, F. J., and Dickson, W. J. *Management and the Worker.* Cambridge, Mass.: Harvard University Press, 1939.

Rogers, C. R. *Client-Centered Therapy.* Boston: Houghton Mifflin, 1951.

Schachter, S. *The Psychology of Affiliation.* Stanford, Calif.: Stanford University Press, 1959.

Schein, E. H. "The Chinese Indoctrination Program for Prisoners of War." *Psychiatry* 19 (1956) : 149–72.

Schutz, W. C. *FIRO.* New York: Rinehart, 1958.

Seashore, S. *Group Cohesiveness in the Industrial Workgroup.* Ann Arbor, Mich.: Institute for Social Research, 1954.

Seidman, J. *Union Rights and Union Duties.* New York: Harcourt, Brace, 1943.

Sherif, M., and Sherif, Carolyn. *Groups in Harmony and Tension.* New York: Harper and Bros., 1953.

Slichter, S. H. *Union Policies and Industrial Management.* Washington, D.C.: The Brookings Institution, 1941.

Stouffer, S. A., et al. *The American Soldier.* Vol. 1. Princeton, N.J.: Princeton University Press, 1949.

Thibaut, J., and Coules, J. "The Role of Communication in the Reduction of Interpersonal Hostility." *Journal of Abnormal and Social Psychology* 47 (1952) : 770–77.

Thibaut, J. W., and Kelley, H. H. *The Social Psychology of Groups.* New York: John Wiley & Sons, 1959.

Thomas, E. J. "Effects of Facilitative Role Interdependence on Group Functioning." *Human Relations* 10 (1957) : 347–66.

Trist, E. L., and Bamforth, K. W. "Some Social and Psychological Consequences of the Longwall Method of Coal Getting." *Human Relations* 54 (1951) : 1–38.

Turner, R. H., and Killian, L. N. *Collective Behavior.* Englewood Cliffs, N.J.: Prentice Hall, 1957.

Van Bergen, Annie, and Koekebakker, J. "Group Cohesiveness in Laboratory Experiments." *Acta Psychologica* 16 (1959) : 81–98.

Vroom, V. H. "Industrial Social Psychology." In *The Handbook of Social Psychology,* edited by G. Lindzey and E. Aronson, vol. 5, pp. 196–268. Reading, Mass.: Addison Wesley, 1969.

————. *Work and Motivation.* New York: John Wiley & Sons, 1964.

Walker, C., and Guest, H. *The Man on the Assembly Line.* Cambridge, Mass.: Harvard University Press, 1952.

Walker, C., Guest, H., and Turner, A. N. *The Foreman on the Assembly Line.* Cambridge, Mass.: Harvard University Press, 1956.

Weller, L. "The Affects of Anxiety on Cohesiveness and Rejection." *Human Relations* 16 (1963) : 189–97.

Whyte, W. F. *Money and Motivation*. New York: Harper and Bros., 1955.

———. *Organizational Behavior: Theory and Application*. Homewood, Ill.: Richard D. Irwin and Dorsey Press, 1969.

INDEX

DATE DUE

APR 13 '78			
SEP 13 '82			
GAYLORD			PRINTED IN U.S.A.